HOME DECORATING WITH
PAINT, TILE, WALLCOVERING

CREATIVE HOMEOWNER PRESS®

CONTENTS

Based on *Creating a Home*,
First Edition © Eaglemoss Publications Limited 1986, 1987, 1988

Printed at Webcrafters, Inc.,
Madison, Wisconsin, U.S.A.

Current printing (last digit)
10 9 8 7 6 5 4 3 2 1

Creative Director: Warren Ramezzana
Editor: Kimberly Kerrigone
Copy Editor: Carolyn Anderson-Feighner
Cover Photograph: Parsekian/Gensheimer
Cover Interior Designer: Barbara Ostrum Associates
Design Consultant: Eve Ardia, ASID, Saddle River Interiors

Library of Congress Catalog Number: 91-071690
ISBN 0-932944-96-5 (paper)

CREATIVE HOMEOWNER PRESS® BOOK SERIES
A DIVISION OF FEDERAL MARKETING CORP.
24 PARK WAY
UPPER SADDLE RIVER, NJ 07458-2311

INTRODUCTION

Decorating the home yourself can be richly rewarding. Not only does it save money, it gives you a unique opportunity to exercise your practical and creative skills.

This book shows how to master basic skills, then develop them to be adventurous in the way you decorate your home. All the techniques are explained in easy-to-follow, step-by-step form, with numerous drawings and photographs illustrating the wonderful effects that you can achieve. Every project includes a 'shopping list' of tools and materials to make sure that you have everything you need before beginning.

The sections on preparation, painting and hanging wallcovering show how to get professional results with a minimum of effort. Guides to choosing paints and wallcoverings include all the latest developments so you can be sure of picking the best product for your purpose. And the chapters on ceramic tiling start off with step-by-step instructions for making a simple backsplash before proceeding on to tackling a kitchen countertop or retiling a bathroom.

In this book you'll find a rich source of ideas for unusual ways of decorating: not only walls, ceilings and woodwork, but furniture too. There are chapters devoted to the popular traditional decorative techniques such as marbling, ragging, color washing and shading, spattering, dragging and combing. Or you can create your own patterns by stenciling, painting a mural, or covering your walls with pleated fabric.

Home Decorating with Paint, Tile, Wallcovering is full of bright ideas for creative original touches, speeding up the work and saving money. It is a must for everyone who wants to do their own decorating with a special flair.

PREPARING WALLS

Take the time to prepare the surface thoroughly and you'll be repaid with a finish that looks good and lasts.

The ideal surface for a decorative finish – paint, wallcovering or tile – is one that is flat, clean and dry. Dirt and grease will prevent any decorative finish from sticking properly.

The preparatory work that is necessary will depend on the condition of existing surfaces as well as the finish intended for it.

New Walls Wallboard is used for the surface of most interior walls built today. Also known as plasterboard, drywall, gypsum board, or by the trade name Sheetrock, wallboard is easy to handle, goes up quickly, and costs relatively little. It provides a surface that can be paneled or tiled, painted or wallpapered.

In order to finish wallboard so that you can paint or wallpaper over it, the unsightly seams and nails that are showing must be smoothed over with a thick spreadable substance called joint compound and paper tape. Taping and plastering will hide a multitude of missed hammer strokes and badly fitting joints.

Joint compound must be applied at least three times and left to dry about 24 hours after each application.

Painted walls For many painted surfaces a thorough cleaning is all that is required before painting or papering. If there are cracks and holes they should be filled, and any mold growth should be destroyed.

Textured paint finishes can be painted over but must be removed if you want to use any other material. If the finish is a textured latex, you can soften it with a steam stripper.

Otherwise you will have to use a chemical paint remover.

Papered walls Avoid papering or painting over old wallcoverings – the dyes in the old covering may bleed through fresh paint, and adhesive for a new wallcovering may pull both old and new coverings from the wall.

Only leave it if the paper is well stuck to the wall or the wallboard beneath is in such poor condition that it might pull away if you strip the surface (test a small patch first). Prime before painting or hanging lining paper for a new wallcovering.

Making the best of it Surfaces that you cannot make smooth but are otherwise sound benefit from a covering of lining paper. Relief papers and textured paint are also useful for disguising uneven and cracked walls.

Before you start Preparatory work is a messy business, so clear away as many furnishings as possible and pile the rest in the middle of the room under drop cloths. Take down curtains and protect the floor with plastic sheeting.

A perfect finish

A successful decorating job – like this one – depends on thorough preparation of the wall surfaces.

TOOLS AND EQUIPMENT

A sponge or a rough cloth is necessary for washing down surfaces. Use a scrubbing brush on textured paint finishes.

Soap or a household detergent will remove dirt and grease from painted surfaces. You will also need a bucket.

Sandpaper – use for painted surfaces and for smoothing filled areas. It is useful to have three grades – fine, medium and coarse.

A sanding block helps to give an even finish – improvise by wrapping sandpaper around a block of wood.

Textured-paint remover may be necessary to remove a textured finish. This can, however, be very expensive.

Wallcovering stripper is used when soaking wallcovering for stripping.

A steam stripper can be rented from a tool rental shop to speed up the process of stripping textured paint and layers of old wallpaper.

A flat scraper with a broad blade is used for stripping wallcovering and paint.

A stiff wire brush, or a scraper with a serrated wire edge, is used to score stubborn wallcoverings before soaking with water.

All-purpose spackle is available ready-mixed for filling small cracks and holes. Use an interior grade.

A filling knife with a narrow flexible blade is necessary for filling cracks and holes in wallboard.

A hammer and cold chisel is useful for removing damaged plaster.

A trowel with a thin flexible blade is necessary for applying spackle.

Plaster finish is essential as a topcoat for new plaster. It comes ready-mixed, and a plastic spreader for application is usually supplied.

An old, clean paintbrush is useful for cleaning out cracks and holes, and dusting off surfaces.

Household bleach, or a mold killer, is essential for destroying mold on wall surfaces.

You will also need drop cloths and plastic sheeting to protect vulnerable surfaces.

SAFETY

When using water to soak walls, make sure the water doesn't run down behind light switches and outlets. Turn off the main switch.

A practical alternative when stripping wallcoverings is to loosen the faceplate slightly and strip an area of about 6in. around switch or outlet before soaking the wall. Then cover the area with polyethylene held in place with masking tape to keep it dry.

CHECK YOUR NEEDS
- ☐ Plastic bucket
- ☐ Soap or detergent
- ☐ Sponge, cloth or scrubbing brush
- ☐ Clean cloths for wiping down
- ☐ Sandpaper
- ☐ Sanding block
- ☐ Flat scraper
- ☐ Textured paint remover
- ☐ Protective clothing and rubber gloves
- ☐ Old paintbrushes
- ☐ Washing-up liquid or wallpaper stripper
- ☐ Wire brush or serrated scraper
- ☐ Steam stripper (optional)
- ☐ Spackle compound
- ☐ Narrow filling knife (1in. blade)
- ☐ Hammer and cold chisel
- ☐ All-purpose plaster
- ☐ Wide putty knife (3in. blade)
- ☐ Plasterer's trowel
- ☐ Plaster finish
- ☐ Bleach or mold killer

Clean painted walls
Use a sponge (or soft scrubbing brush for textured finishes) and a solution of warm water and soap or household detergent.

Wash the ceiling first, then the walls, working from the bottom upwards to catch any dirty streaks that run down. Rinse thoroughly with clean water and allow to dry.

Then, if the walls have been painted with gloss, rub them down with wet-and-dry sandpaper to provide a slightly rough surface for new decorations (a fine-grade paper if you're painting: a coarser grade if you are hanging wallcoverings).

Strip textured paint finishes ▷
A steam stripper may soften the paint sufficiently for stripping in the same way as for wallcovering.

If this fails, use a textured-paint remover. Apply it carefully with a brush, and wear rubber gloves and protective clothing to guard against splashes. Leave the remover to penetrate, then strip off the softened material with a flat scraper and rinse the surface thoroughly with cold water.

Remove textured paint
Scrub the walls with a firm scrubbing brush and plenty of warm water, changing the water whenever it becomes cloudy. Rinse down with warm water and let the surface dry.

Then sand smooth and apply a primer if you are painting or a thin coat of size (weak wallcovering paste) if you are hanging wallcovering.

Remove flaking paint △
Use a flat scraper to scrape away small areas of loose flaking paint. Sand the edges of bare patches smooth with fine-grade sandpaper, and paint them with latex before repainting the entire wall.

Strip ordinary wallcovering ▷
Use a sponge or old paintbrush to wet the wall with hot water containing a little detergent or wallcovering stripper (see Safety note). Leave it to soak through the covering and soften the paste beneath.

Then slide a flat scraper under a loose edge and scrape off the covering. Hold the scraper firmly and keep it as flat to the wall as possible so that you don't dig into the wall. Keep resoaking the paper until it comes off easily. To avoid spreading soggy paper around, gather strippings as you go.

Strip washable or painted paper △
If wallpaper has a water-resistant finish the surface must be broken before sponging to allow the water to soak through. Use a stiff wire brush or a serrated scraper to score the paper, taking care not to damage the surface beneath.

Steam stripper △
You can hire a steam stripper from your local rental shop. This machine forces steam into the paper and speeds up the process of softening the paste – the paper is then scraped off as for ordinary wallcovering. Be sure to follow the rental shop's instructions.

Strip vinyl wallcoverings △
Peel the top vinyl layer off the backing paper that is stuck to the wall – lift a corner seam with your fingernail at baseboard level. Loosen the bottom edge from the wall and pull upwards to remove it completely. You can paint or paper over the backing paper as long as it is firmly stuck to the wall, but for a thorough job it is best to strip it.

◁ **Strip for action**
It really is worth putting the time into preparing your wall surfaces properly. After all, the final finish can only be as smooth as the surface beneath it.

This room is being stripped back to the basics. Unless old wallcovering is really well stuck to the wall, or the plaster beneath it is in very poor condition, the old paper should be removed before redecorating with new paint or wallcoverings.

Getting rid of old wallcoverings usually depends on soaking the walls thoroughly with water so that the adhesive behind the paper begins to dissolve. This is a messy job so clear out as much furniture as possible, take down curtains and, if possible, remove the floorcovering as well.

Clean up a stripped surface △

Once all the paper has been removed, rub off any small remnants of paper with coarse-grade sandpaper wrapped around a wood block. Then wash the whole wall with detergent solution to remove old pastes, rub down with fine sandpaper and dust off.

Fill small cracks and holes ▷

Most minor cracks and holes can be dealt with using an interior general-purpose spackle. A badly cracked ceiling, however, can be difficult to fill satisfactorily – wallcovering or textured paint may be a better answer than filling.

Use an all-purpose filler to fill small cracks and holes in walls. First rake out loose material from cracks with the edge of a putty knife and dust off with an old paintbrush. If working with plaster walls, wet the plaster with a sponge to stop the repair from drying out too quickly (a houseplant sprayer comes in handy!).

For cracks, draw the blade across and then along the crack to force the spackle well in. Fill a deep crack or hole in 2 or 3 layers of no more than ¼in.

thickness, allowing each layer to dry hard before applying the next one. Always overfill the crack or hole – you can rub off the excess with sandpaper once it has dried. Then dust clean with an old paintbrush.

Repair damaged plaster △

Larger holes and damaged areas up to 12in. square should be repaired with all-purpose plaster and a plaster finish. Leave larger areas of plasterwork to a professional.

Remove damaged material using a hammer and cold chisel (left), working from the center outwards until you reach a sound point. Then repair the patch with all-purpose plaster built up in at least two layers to within about ⅛in. of the surface.

Stir the plaster, then apply it to the wall with a trowel or large putty knife (right). Push the plaster firmly against the wall and spread it smooth, moving the trowel steadily upwards with the blade at an angle of about 45 degrees to the surface. When the first layer begins to harden, roughen up the surface with wire or a nail to provide a base for the next layer.

Apply the plaster finish △

Leave the undercoat of plaster for at least 24 hours to dry thoroughly before applying a thin 'skim' coat of plaster finish. Stir the plaster until creamy and apply it evenly to the wall using a large paintbrush and light upward strokes.

Then smooth over with the flexible plastic spreader provided. Keep working the surface with the spreader until you are satisfied that the finish is smooth. If necessary, dip the spreader into water and slightly dampen the plaster – but just enough to remove any ridges and marks.

TREATING MOLD

Mold growth – usually black or dark brown splotches on wall surfaces – is encouraged by dampness and condensation. In these conditions it can spread rapidly – by airborn spores or even by contact with cleaning cloths that have been previously infected.

Mold can be treated with a solution of household bleach, or with a mold killer (following the manufacturer's instructions). This will destroy mold but you should also try to take action to avoid reinfection. Increasing heat or insulation and improving ventilation, for example, may be the simplest solutions to a condensation problem.

Household bleach To use household bleach, make up a solution of 1 part bleach to 5 parts water. Brush it onto infected and surrounding areas and leave to soak overnight. Then scrape off the mold, and burn all the scrapings. Rinse the surface with clean water and apply a fresh bleach solution. Leave for at least three days before decorating.

For mold on wallcoverings, remove the infected paper before treating the wall with bleach solution. Use a fungicidal paste when hanging new paper.

After treating mold, sterilize cleaning equipment with bleach.

TOUCH UP FILLED AREAS

A patch of filler or an area of new plaster will absorb far more paint than the surrounding surface area of old plaster or plasterboard. The patched areas will appear slightly gray under a fresh coat of paint.

To avoid this, seal the repair with primer or one or two coats of latex paint before painting the entire wall.

See Interior Paints, pages 11-12, for information on choosing primers and paints for interior use.

INTERIOR PAINTS

Paint is a decorative and long-lasting protective finish for almost any surface – as long as you choose the right paint for the job.

This chapter deals with paint for indoors, where it is mainly used as a decorative finish. There are situations, however, where special qualities are needed: paint on kitchen and bathroom walls, for example, has to stand up to condensation and be easy to clean.

Apart from color, there are two major factors to bear in mind when choosing paint – the type and the finish.

TYPES OF PAINT
Paints are divided into two basic categories: water-based and oil-based paints. The charts below and overleaf tell you where and how to best use them.

Water-based paints (latex) include paints referred to as latex and acrylics.

They are the most simple to work with: no undercoat is required, they are easy to apply, fast-drying, and tools can be cleaned in water. Most latex is washable.

Oil-based paints need careful application, and most require cleaning up with mineral spirits (or similar solvent). They take time to dry, and on bare surfaces both primer and undercoat are essential. They are more expensive but much tougher than latex – they are scrubbable and stand up well to moisture and condensation so are ideal for kitchens and bathrooms.

Depending upon the quality of the latex or oil-based paint, you will need to use one or more coats.

FINISHES
Latex is available in flat, satin, semi-gloss or textured finishes. Oil-based paints range from a subdued sheen to hard, high gloss.

Paints with a shine, including semi-gloss latex, will highlight any surface defects but they are much easier to clean than flat latex.

COLOR
Most paint finishes are available in a huge range of colors – either ready-mixed or custom-mixed from in-store tinting systems. Color squares on shade cards are only an approximation of final paint colors, and they're so small that it is hard to imagine how they will look on an expanse of wall. So, before making a decision, try and get small 'test' pots of the colors you like and experiment. Then you can see how they work and avoid making expensive mistakes.

If you are going to have paint custom-mixed, make sure you buy all you need in one batch – getting a precise color match from a second batch is difficult.

Before splashing out on your tin of paint, check the charts below and on page 12 to find out which paint to buy for the job. If necessary, buy solvent at the same time.

THE RIGHT PAINT FOR THE SURFACE

	PRIMER	UNDERCOAT	TOPCOAT
WALLS/CEILINGS			
New plaster/plasterboard	sealing coat of latex primer	not needed	coat(s) of latex or oil-based paint
	do not use oil-based paint on plaster that has not dried out thoroughly		
Sound painted plaster	thinned coat of latex on bare areas	not needed	coat(s) of latex or oil-based paint
	do not use latex over gloss paint, without first sanding the surface thoroughly		
Wallcovering/anaglypta	sealing coat of latex	only under high gloss	coat(s) of latex or oil-based paint
Embossed tin	sealing coat of oil-based primer	only under high gloss	coat(s) of latex or oil-based paint
Glazed tiles	thinned coat of oil-based high gloss paint (9 parts paint: 1 part mineral spirits)	do not use undercoat	1 coat of oil-based high gloss paint
WOOD			
Bare softwood/building boards	knotting over resinous streaks or knots, then oil-based wood primer	only under high gloss	coat(s) of latex or oil-based paint
Bare hardwood	oil-based wood primer	only under high gloss	coat(s) of latex or oil-based paint
Sound painted wood	not needed	only under high gloss	coat(s) of latex or oil-based paint
METAL			
New galvanized iron (some window frames, for example)	quick-drying metal primer	undercoat	coat(s) of latex or oil-based paint
Radiators	quick-drying metal primer on bare metal	do not use undercoat	2 coats of latex or oil-based paint

CHOOSING THE RIGHT PAINT

TYPE	USES	ADVANTAGES	WATCH POINTS	SOLVENT/THINNER
Primer Types include: all-purpose oil-based wood latex wood quick-drying metal	Essential on new wood and metal. All-purpose primer is suitable for most surfaces around the home. Other primers available for specific uses.	Seals the surface and provides a base for next coat. Primer on its own is not permanent protection – cover with undercoat and topcoat immediately after specified drying time.		mineral spirits (oil-based and metal) or water
Undercoat oil-based latex	Use after primer when building up a paint system on new wood or metal, or on old paint job when changing color significantly.	Designed to have good covering power; can easily be rubbed smooth ready for a top coat.	Undercoat, like primer, must be painted over as quickly as possible.	mineral spirits (oil-based) or water (latex)
WATER-BASED PAINTS				
Flat latex	For walls and ceilings. Being water-based they allow surface to breathe, so use on new plaster or porous surfaces such as rough brickwork.	Covers well; reflects light so will not highlight imperfections on uneven walls. Inexpensive, easy to apply, fast drying (recoatable in about 4 hours), and washable.	Shows scuff marks and likely to develop sheen with washing, so best used in areas of light wear such as bedrooms, living rooms, dining rooms.	soap and water/water
Satin latex	For walls and ceilings – as for flat latex.	Tougher and more washable than flat latex. Particularly effective on relief papers and other textured wallcoverings. Cheap, easy to apply, fast drying (recoatable in about 4 hours). Solid paint non-drip, so useful for ceilings.	Will highlight irregular surfaces.	soap and water/water
Textured latex	For walls and ceilings.	Gives a rough-stone or sandy finish good for disguising imperfect walls.	Difficult to wash and very difficult to remove.	soap and water/water
Semi-gloss	Interior woodwork.	Easier to apply than oil-based gloss (recoatable in about 6 hours).	Not as hardwearing nor as shiny as oil-based gloss.	soap and water/water
OIL-BASED PAINTS				
Flat Satin	All-purpose paint for walls and ceilings, wood and metal. Ideal for areas of heavy condensation such as kitchens and bathrooms, and also for metal radiators and tin ceilings.	Tougher than latex and more subtle than high gloss. Wears well and very washable. Normally needs no undercoat (though bare surfaces should be primed) and needs less brushing out than gloss.	More expensive than latex. Takes 12-16 hours to dry and needs more careful application than latex.	mineral spirits
High gloss	For surfaces that need maximum protection – kitchen cabinets, window sills and wood floors.	Easy to clean and hardwearing. Applied quite thickly, which can mean fewer coats and good covering power. High gloss flows on evenly and is particularly good for difficult surfaces such as window frames and moldings.	Takes 12-16 hours to dry. The shiny finish highlights surface flaws, so thorough preparation is necessary. High gloss is more difficult to use for beginners, needs an undercoat.	mineral spirits

PAINTING WALLS AND CEILINGS

Brighten up your room with a fresh coat of paint. Or give it a completely new look by sponging on a decorative paint finish in two or more colors.

Painting is the easiest, the least expensive and the most versatile way of giving a room new life.

Paints are available in several finishes and there are literally hundreds of colors to choose from. This chapter deals with water-based latex paints and oil-based paints suitable for painting walls and ceilings. Use them for either plain or decorative finishes.

Sponging is the simplest decorative paint treatment to try first.

Where to start Begin with smooth, clean surfaces and your paint job will look better and last longer. If wall surfaces are very poor, you can paper the walls first with a white paper that is intended for painting over – lining paper or relief paper, for example. To get your walls in good shape, see the chapters on Preparing Walls and Hanging Wallcovering.

Before starting to paint, clean the room to remove dust and make sure that vulnerable surfaces are covered with drop cloths or plastic sheeting.

What to paint first If you are painting the whole room, tackle the ceiling first, then the walls and finally the woodwork.

If you're hanging wallcovering, do all your painting first – then there's no worry about splashing the finished walls.

Which paint? Most people opt for latex paint – it's easy to handle and very fast drying. High quality latex is particularly good for ceilings as it doesn't drip.

For kitchens and bathrooms, where condensation may be a problem, an oil-based paint is a practical choice but it requires more careful painting and is slower drying.

See Interior Paints for how to choose the most suitable paint and finish for the job at hand.

How much paint? Two coats of paint are usually sufficient to cover a wall or ceiling. But if the walls are very rough or porous, or you're painting a light color over a dark one, you may need a third coat to get a good finish.

To calculate the area of walls to be painted, multiply the width of each wall by its height and add the totals together. The ceiling area of a room is usually equal to the floor area (multiply the room's length by its width).

Covering capacity varies from one paint brand to the next but, as a rough guide, 1 gallon of latex will cover about 40sq.ft. Check on the paint can and bear in mind the number of coats that will be needed.

Perfect paint job
The walls and ceiling of this bright kitchen are painted with oil-based semi-gloss satin, which is easier to clean than flat waterbase.

WHAT ABOUT TOOLS?

Most paints can be applied with a roller, brush or paint pad.

For latex, a roller is probably the most useful tool for covering large areas such as walls and ceilings quickly. You will, however, still need a brush or paint pad for smaller areas and awkward corners.

Rollers Buy a good quality roller (inexpensive foam gives a poor finish) with a pile to suit the job – short pile for smooth surfaces, a longer pile for textured surfaces such as relief wallcoverings.

There are special rollers with long handles for ceilings but with most standard rollers you can fit an extension (a broom handle is ideal) into the end of the handle.

Brushes These give good results but are slower than rollers. A 4in. wall brush is the best size for painting very large areas and a 2in. brush for filling in edges. Before using a new brush, wash it in warm water and tease out any loose bristles.

Paint pads These are lightweight and won't splash but they can be tricky to load up with paint. An edging pad is very useful for painting between walls and ceilings.

Paint tray You will need a special tray for loading a roller with paint. Paint trays are supplied with some paint pads but a roller tray or a deep can lid will do just as well.

Paint bucket If you're using a brush, a paint bucket (or any shallow, wide-topped container with a handle) is useful for decanting small quantities of paint. It's much easier to work with than a heavy paint can, particularly if you're up a ladder.

Stepladders To reach ceilings and tops of walls, ideally you should rig up a working platform. A plank of wood wedged securely between two stepladders is safer than using a chair that can easily tip over.

Odds and ends Use masking tape (low-tack adhesive tape) for protecting light fixtures, and have plenty of old rags for mopping and cleaning up.

Cleaning tools For cleaning off latex you need plenty of water. It dries fast, so wash your tools as soon as you have finished with them; get rid of excess paint on newspaper before rinsing thoroughly.

Hang brushes up with the bristles loosely held in shape with a rubber band; store flat when dry.

For short breaks – between coats, for instance – keep your tools from drying out by wrapping them in plastic wrap or in a plastic bag sealed with an elastic band.

USING A ROLLER △

(Suitable for latex paints)
Pour some paint into the deep end of the roller tray, leaving the ridged section uncovered. Then dip the roller in the paint and run it back and forth over the ridged slope of the tray to distribute the paint evenly.

Roll the paint onto the wall with criss-cross diagonal strokes to cover a block. Start a second block alongside, avoiding ridges of excess paint by using a thinly coated roller on overlaps.

When painting ceilings, wear goggles for protection and don't let the roller spin freely or it will splash.

USING A BRUSH △

(Suitable for all types of paint)
Before using a new brush, wash it in warm water and tease out any loose bristles. Pour some paint into a bucket if you are using one. Load the brush by dipping just one-third of the bristles into the paint – don't overload the brush or paint may run back over the handle.

Apply paint using vertical strokes first, then change direction to spread paint evenly. Don't apply too much paint where blocks overlap.

USING A PAINT PAD ▷

(Suitable for latex paints)
Pour some paint into a paint pan and thin it with a little water. Hold the pad flat and dip only the mohair pile (never the foam backing) into the paint. Then draw the pad over the edge of the tray to wipe off any excess paint. Apply paint by lightly wiping the pad up and down over the wall surface.

ORDER OF PAINTING ▷

Paint the ceiling first, then the walls. Always start at the window end of a room and work away from the light as shown in the diagram opposite – this makes it easier to see which areas have been painted.

Try to paint a ceiling, or a complete wall, in one shot – if you take a break in the middle, the dried edge may show as a definite mark when you have finished.

1 Prepare to paint
Wipe the lid of the paint can clean of dust before opening it. Then stir the paint thoroughly with a clean wooden stick to shift any thick paint from the bottom.

2 Paint ceiling edges and corners ▷
First paint a narrow margin around the edges and corners of the ceiling using a narrow brush or edging pad.

To use an edging pad press its guide wheels against the wall ceiling junction and roll the pad along to get a sharp clean line. Don't overload the pad and make sure the wheels are paint free.

3 Fill in the main ceiling area ▷
Start in a corner at the window end of the room and work in manageable strips (about 1 yard wide) across the ceiling.

Ideally work from a platform (see checklist), a stepladder, or fit an extension handle to a roller so that you can paint the ceiling from the floor.

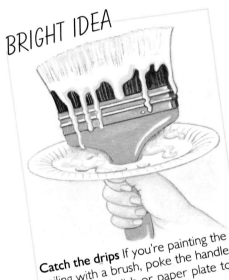

BRIGHT IDEA

Catch the drips If you're painting the ceiling with a brush, poke the handle through a foil dish or paper plate to catch the drips.

4 Paint around features △
Paint along the edges of molding, around window frames, light switches, etc., before you start to paint the main wall area. Use a small paint pad or a narrow brush (held sideways as shown).

Using an oil-based paint on walls ▷
Oil-based paint requires careful application (it's stickier and slower drying than latex) and you will get best results by using a brush. (Rollers and pads tend to leave marks.)

Apply the paint using criss-cross strokes as for latex, but finish off each section with light upward strokes to smooth out brush marks. Brush marks will show if you overlap dry paint so it's important to keep a wet edge around blocks.

Store brushes for short periods between painting by immersing just the bristles in water; shake out the water before using again.

When you have finished painting, clean your tools in mineral spirits or paintbrush cleaner, then wash in warm soapy water and rinse.

5 Paint the walls
Start at the top right-hand corner of a wall (top left if left-handed) and work across in horizontal bands from the ceiling downwards. This way you will be able to paint over any drips.

If small bubbles appear when painting over paper, leave them until the paint dries. Most will disappear but use a sharp razor blade to slit any that remain with a cross. Dab some wallpaper paste behind and flatten the paper. Retouch with paint when the area is completely dry.

15

SPONGING

Sponging is fun and fast to do, using flat, satin, or semi-gloss water-base paints. By simply sponging on one or more toning or contrasting colors over a plain painted base you can create a pretty 'speckled egg' effect on your walls. A bright or pastel color over white, for example, looks crisp and fresh, a light and dark tone of the same color gives a more subtle effect – or try several colors such as pink, peach and cream over a yellow base. The results are infinitely variable, depending on the number of colors and the size and spacing of your sponge marks.

Use paint straight from the can for strong prints, or dilute it with a little water to make softer marks.

Materials The only special equipment you need is a natural sea sponge of a size that fits comfortably in your hand.

You will also need a shallow dish for moistening the sponge with paint, and a spoon for transferring paint from the can. Have plenty of scrap paper handy for testing prints (the back of leftover pieces of lining paper or wallcovering is ideal), and plenty of old rags for wiping up as you go along.

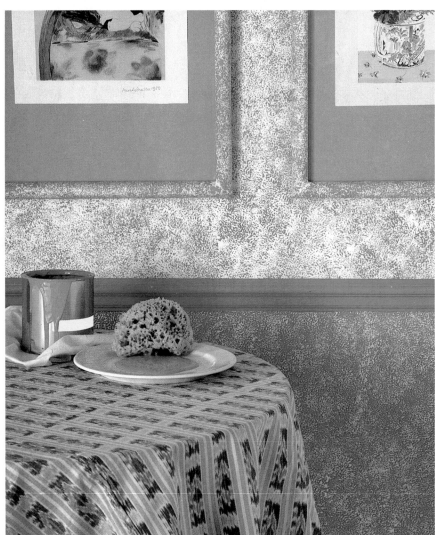

1 *Apply the base color*
Paint the walls with the base color and allow it to dry for at least 24 hours.

2 *Using the sponge △*
First, wet the sponge then wring it out so that it's just damp. Spoon about a tablespoon of the sponging color into the shallow dish. Then either dip the flat side of the sponge into the paint or brush color evenly onto the sponge with a paintbrush.

Two-tone sponging ▽
Slightly denser sponging below the chair rail contrasts with the lighter stipple above it. Even the picture frames are decorated with this attractive finish.

3 *Test the print △*
Gently pat the sponge onto the scrap paper. Splotchy wet prints mean that the sponge is overloaded with paint – keep dabbing until it leaves a soft, speckled mark.

4 *Sponge the wall △*
Starting at a corner, lightly dab sponge prints over the wall – turning the sponge around every so often to vary the mark it makes. Use a small piece of sponge to get into corners and a damp cloth to wipe off any smudges.

When the print gets faint, recharge the sponge with paint but always test the print first on paper. If the sponge gets clogged up, wipe it clean on rags or rinse in water.

5 *Sponge on two or more colors △*
If you're using several colors, space your first prints so that a good bit of base color shows through. When the first sponged color is dry, apply the second color – then more if you wish. Fill gaps, but overlap prints too so that colors mingle.

6 *Check the finish*
Stand back now and then to judge the effect. If you've sponged on too much paint in places, it can be lightened once the paint is dry by sponging on a little base color.

PREPARING AND PAINTING WOODWORK

Painting woodwork is not difficult but these surfaces get a lot of hard wear, so good preparation is a must.

Bright, freshly painted woodwork – from windows and doors to staircases and molding – adds greatly to the appearance of a newly decorated room.

This chapter covers preparing and painting woodwork with oil-based paints. Carefully applied, these paints give a durable finish that is easy to keep clean.

Check the wood is sound If wood is rotting badly, there's no point in redecorating. Unsound wood is usually warped and has a broken surface. Stick a sharp pointed tool (a small screwdriver will do) into any suspect areas – if the blade goes in easily in several places, call in a specialist to investigate.

Preparing woodwork An old paint job that is sound only needs washing down, and a little filling and sanding to hide small cracks and nail holes. Only strip paint if it is peeling or blistering badly, or if there is a thick build-up of old paint.

New wood needs to be sanded smooth, and knots sealed with a shellac sealer to prevent resin from bleeding through subsequent layers of paint.

When to paint woodwork Prepare the woodwork at the same time as any other surfaces to be decorated. Paint the woodwork after you've done the walls and ceiling, but before you lay new flooring.

Paint windows first, then any cupboards or shelves, then doors, and finally the baseboard.

WHICH PAINT?
High-gloss paint gives the toughest finish but reveals imperfections. If the surface is a bit rough, a gloss or matte finish may be preferable.

Starting from scratch New wood requires a wood primer first, then an

Neat paint job
Gloss paint, carefully applied, enhances the attractive woodwork in this traditional entrance hall.

undercoat in a color to suit the topcoat. With gloss and semi-gloss paints undercoat is not always necessary.

Existing paint jobs One topcoat is usually enough but, if you're painting a light color over a dark one, you may need undercoat and two topcoats to get a good finish. (See Interior Paints for suitable types of paints.)

HOW MUCH PAINT?

Covering capacity varies from one paint brand to the next – as a rough guide, a door takes about 3 ounces for each coat.

TOOLS AND EQUIPMENT

Sandpaper to smooth surfaces and provide a base for new paint. Use sandpaper on new wood. For sanding down an existing paint job, paper is useful in fine, medium and coarse grades.

A sanding block Wrap sandpaper around a block of wood or cork when sanding a flat surface. For moldings, wrap paper around a sponge instead.

A scraper to remove loose or blistering paint.

Ready-mixed wood filler to cover surface dents and small holes.

Interior-grade cellulose filler to fill cracks and holes deeper than ¼in. or open joints (e.g., between baseboard and the wall). It comes as powder to be mixed with water.

Paintbrushes A 3in. brush for large areas; a 2in. brush for panels and molding. A 1½in. cutting-in brush with angled bristles is useful for painting straight lines, up to corners and awkward edges.

Masking tape for protecting surfaces when painting straight lines.

A shield is useful when painting up to edges – use a piece of stiff cardboard, or buy a special plastic or metal paint shield.

CHECK YOUR NEEDS
- ☐ Oil-based paint
- ☐ Primer (on new or bare wood)
- ☐ Undercoat (optional)
- ☐ 3in. or 4in. paintbrush
- ☐ 2in. paintbrush
- ☐ 1½in. cutting-in brush
- ☐ Masking tape, paint shield
- ☐ Mineral spirits or paint brush cleaner/restorer
- ☐ Drop cloths and newspaper for protecting surfaces
- ☐ Cleaning up rags

Preparation details:
- ☐ Soap or household detergent
- ☐ Plastic bucket
- ☐ Sponge or cloth
- ☐ Rubber gloves
- ☐ Sandpaper
- ☐ Sanding block
- ☐ Scraper
- ☐ All-purpose cellulose filler
- ☐ Filling knife (or old table knife)
- ☐ Shellac sealer, hair dryer

TAKING CARE OF PAINTBRUSHES

Before using a new brush, wash it in warm water and tease out any loose bristles.

After use, wipe excess paint on newspaper, then clean the brush in turpentine or mineral spirits. Wash in warm soapy water and rinse well.

Soak an old, hardened brush in paint brush cleaner before washing – if bristles remain stuck together, throw it away.

Store brushes during breaks by immersing just the bristles in water; shake out the water before using again. To stop bristles from being bent out of shape, use a nail and string to suspend the brush over a jar.

1 Wash painted walls
Wash down old paint job with a sponge and solution of warm water and soap or household detergent to remove dirt and grease. Rinse with clean water and leave to dry.

2 Sand down △
Sand old paint job lightly along the grain to remove the shine and provide a base for new paint. Use fine-grade sandpaper wrapped around a sanding block, and sprinkled with soapy water.

Dust off, then wipe over paint job with a cloth dipped in mineral spirits and leave to dry.

New wood Sand down along the grain of the wood with medium then fine-grade sandpaper, and round off sharp edges. Remove surface dust with a cloth dampened with mineral spirits.

3 Remove loose paint
Remove small areas of loose or blistered paint with a scraper, keeping the blade as flat to the surface as possible. Take back to bare wood if necessary, and rub down the edges of the stripped patch with coarse-grade sandpaper until flush.

4 Fill dents, holes and joints
Fill nicks and dents with fine surface filler; fill larger holes with spackle. Dab oil-based paint onto nail and screw heads before covering.

Apply spackle with a putty knife or an old table knife and level off by drawing the blade across the surface. When dry, rub smooth with fine-grade sandpaper.

For awkward gaps, pack spackle in with your finger (wearing a rubber glove) and wipe over immediately with a damp rag to smooth the surface.

5 Seal knots in bare wood △
If there are lots of knots in bare wood, heat each knot with a hair dryer to draw out the resin. Let this dry, then scrape away the resin and seal the knot by painting on two thin coats of shellac sealer.

6 Apply primer/undercoat
First, prime new wood (and any bare or filled patches in a painted surface) with a thin coat of primer. Leave to dry thoroughly, then gently rub smooth with fine-grade sandpaper.

After priming, apply undercoat if you are using high-gloss paint or if you are changing the existing color radically. Brush on one coat and leave to dry.

7 Prepare to paint ▷
Wipe the lid of the paint can clean of dust before removing it. If stirring the paint is recommended (check on the can), use a clean wooden stick in a figure-eight motion to shift pigment from the bottom of the can.

If a thick skin has formed on paint already opened, cut around the outside of it with a sharp knife and remove it in one piece if possible before stirring. When you

load your brush, dip just one-third of the bristles into the paint. Avoid getting paint in the metal ferrule of the handle or it may drip.

8 Painting large areas △
Paint blocks 12-18in. square and join these up as you go along. Apply paint along the grain of the wood, then brush back and forth across the grain to produce an even layer of paint. Lastly, stroke the paint gently along the grain to get a smooth finish.

Keep paint thin where blocks overlap to avoid ridges forming, and always work against a 'wet' block so that you can blend in the fresh paint.

To prevent a build-up of paint on the edge of a door, for example, always brush out towards the edge – not in from it.

KEEP THE CAN CLEAN
To prevent dribbles and build-up of paint around the rim, tape or tie a length of string across the top of the can and use this to remove excess paint from the brush. Alternatively, you can buy a special plastic ring to fit onto the top of a 1 gallon can.

9 Painting small areas
Use a 2in. brush to apply paint in a series of dabs about 2½in. apart, then join them up.

Cover narrow sections, such as the muntins of windows, by simply stroking the paint along the grain of the wood.

10 Painting straight edges △
When painting along edges such as baseboards or window frames, protect the floor or glass with masking tape. Peel it off glass as soon as the paint is dry – otherwise it is difficult to remove.

Alternatively, protect the surface by holding a piece of stiff cardboard or a paint shield. Wipe it clean of paint each time it's moved to a new position.

Cutting in Where you can't or don't want to use tape or a shield, use a cutting-in brush with angled bristles to paint a straight edge, or adapt an ordinary narrow brush.

Load the brush lightly and hold it as shown. Slowly push it in to meet the join, then press lightly and draw it along firmly to make a straight line.

BRIGHT IDEA

PAINT A SHARP EDGE
Adapt an ordinary narrow brush for cutting in (or make an angled brush even more effective) by wrapping an elastic band around the bristles to stop them splaying out too much.

ORDER OF PAINTING: WINDOWS

Unscrew all fastenings, and open the window when painting.

When painting the rebates (where wood and glass meet), run a thin line of paint onto the glass to seal the putty. Any paint smudges can be scraped off when dry with a razor blade; use nail polish remover to take off paint on reeded glass.

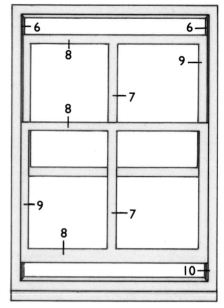

Casement windows △
Begin with *1* the inside edge of the frame and *2* the opening edge of the window. Then paint *3* all the rebates, *4* the muntins, *5-6* the top and bottom horizontal rails, *7* the hinged stile, *8* the meeting stile, and last, *9* the window frame and sill.

Do not close the window until the paint is completely dry.

Double-hung windows △
Raise the bottom sash and pull the top sash down, so that you can paint the meeting rail (including its rebate and bottom edge).

Then paint as much as you can of *2* the muntins (including the rebates) and stiles on the upper sash, *3* the bottom edge of the lower sash, *4* the inside edge of the frame, and *5* a short way down the outside runners.

Leave paint to dry, then reposition the window as shown (closing it almost completely) and paint *6* what you can of the inside runners. Then paint *7* all the rebates and muntins, *8* the remaining cross rails, and *9* the stiles. Last, paint *10* the window frame, architrave and sill.

Make sure you do not paint the sash cords.

ORDER OF PAINTING: DOORS

Unscrew and remove all fittings apart from the hinges. Wedge the door open with a block of wood, and slide a paper bag or newspaper underneath to protect the floor.
Paint the edges of a flush or panel door before you paint the face of it or the frame. With the door opening towards you, paint the opening edge; with it opening away, paint the hinged edge. Unless you can see a door from above, there's no need to paint the top of it.

Flush doors ◁
Paint a flat door in sections about 16in. square using a 3in. brush. Start at the top and work quickly across the door, then down it in bands. Paint the door frame last, and leave the door ajar until dry.

Panel doors ▷
Begin with the inset panels *1-4*, painting each panel immediately after its molding.

Next paint the central vertical section *5-6*, then the horizontal sections *7-9* (top bar, middle bar, then the bottom one). Then paint the outer vertical sections *10-11*.

Last, paint the door frame.

SPECIAL EFFECTS WITH PAINT

Ragging, rag-rolling or stippling: these paint techniques create a wonderful variety of effects, and they're fun and easy to do.

A broken color finish is an exciting alternative to plainly painted walls, and most will actually help to disguise any minor imperfections in the surface.

Ragging, rag-rolling and stippling all involve painting a top 'glaze' coat over a lighter base coat, then breaking up the wet glaze in some way to give depth and texture to the surface.

The techniques are straightforward, but you do have to work fast: on large surfaces such as walls it's best if two people work together.

Ragging and rag-rolling produce a bold, rich texture like crushed velvet, using bunched-up rags that are pressed into or rolled over the wet glaze. It looks good on a large scale, and is quite quick to do.

You'll need a large supply of rags as they soon get soaked with paint. Old sheets make good lint-free rags; for different effects try well-washed hessian, cheesecloth, paper, or even plastic bags.

Stippling gives a very subtle, fine-textured finish with a soft-bristled brush used to lift off just enough color for the background to show through. Time consuming and fairly tiring on a large scale, it looks good on woodwork and furniture as well as walls: the method is the same.

For best results you can buy special stippling brushes made of fine bristle, but these are very expensive. You can improvise fairly successfully with a painter's dusting brush, or a soft-bristled broom or old clothes brush as long as it has a blunt, level surface.

Color schemes Although the tone of the top glaze coat is the dominating one, the color you choose for the base coat influences the finished effect. A white base gives soft, glowing color; for a richer look, try a pastel-colored base and pick a darker tone for the glaze. With ragging or rag-rolling, you can achieve subtle effects by using two slightly different but harmonious colors on top of each other.

Whichever finish you choose, experiment with different color schemes and practice the technique on pre-painted board or cardboard until you feel happy with the effect. The more you practice, the better the results.

PREPARATION

Surfaces to be painted should be clean and sound. Although slightly bumpy walls are less obvious with a ragged or stippled finish, the ideal surface is smooth and even.

For basic preparation tasks, see Preparing Walls, pages 7-10; walls that are very shabby but otherwise sound are best covered with lining paper, see Hanging Wallcovering, pages 61-64.

Then paint on the base coat and leave to dry thoroughly, allowing up to 24 hours before applying the glaze coat.

Ragged looks ▽
This finish – using a warm terra-cotta base, ragged with a transparent burnt sienna – makes a striking background for deep mahogany bedroom furniture.

WHICH PAINT?

The base coat One or two coats of flat oil-based paint is ideal: the result is a smooth, non-absorbent base over which the glaze slides easily and doesn't sink in. Matte or satin finishes don't normally require undercoat, but prime any bare surfaces.

Satin latex is a reasonable substitute and, being water-based, it's easier to apply. You'll probably need to apply two coats for good coverage.

The glaze coat The traditional glaze is semi-transparent – based on a transparent oil glaze (or scumble glaze) that is tinted to the right color and thinned with mineral spirits to a workable consistency. It dries slowly, so that you have enough time to work on the finish, and holds the decorative patterns distinctly.

Depending on the brand, transparent oil glaze ranges from off-white to a deep gold color when looked at in the can. When brushed out it goes transparent but does tend to yellow slightly with age. Available from specialist paint shops; about half a quart glazes a small room.

Tinting Transparent oil glaze can be dyed with universal tints, which are cheap, strong and come in basic colors, or artists' oil colors, which are more expensive but are available in a huge range of shades. Universal tints are sold at most paint shops; artists' oils by art shops.

For light shades, mix the tinting colors into a base of white satin paint. This makes the glaze more opaque, and softens the effect of the decorative finish.

WAYS OF WORKING

On large surfaces such as walls, these finishes are easier and much less tiring if two people work together.

One person applies a strip of glaze, the other follows closely behind and starts treating it before it dries; meanwhile, the first painter begins applying another strip of glaze. The trick is to keep out of each other's way but with a little practice you'll soon get a good, speedy rhythm going – essential for a successful finish.

It's a good idea to start off on a window wall where any beginner's mistakes will be less noticeable.

Always paint at least a whole wall in one session, stopping if necessary at a corner. If you stop in the middle of a wall, the dried edge may show as a definite join when you've finished.

CHECK YOUR NEEDS

For the base coat:
☐ Oil-based paint
  (prime bare surfaces first)
☐ Roller and pan

For the glaze coat:
☐ Transparent oil glaze
☐ Mineral spirits
☐ White plastic paint pail

For tinting the glaze:
☐ Universal tint/artists'
  oil color
☐ White oil-based paint (for
  light colors)
☐ Saucer or bowl
☐ Narrow long-handled paintbrush for mixing
☐ Old spoon
☐ Scrap paper for testing

For the finish:
☐ Paintbrush for applying glaze
☐ White cotton rags, about 16in.
  square, for ragging/rag-rolling
  OR
  Stippling brush (or painter's
  dusting brush, soft-bristled
  broom or clothes brush)
☐ Stepladder for tops of walls
☐ Plastic sheets/newspaper
☐ Rags for mopping up
☐ Rubber gloves

SAFETY
Rags soaked in paint and solvent are highly flammable: let them dry out completely before disposing of them carefully.

1 Tint the glaze △
Tinting glaze to exactly the right shade is a matter of experimenting so use small amounts of dye – artists' oil colors or universal tints – at a time (a couple of inches squeezed from the tube is plenty). Aim to mix enough glaze for the whole room, but keep a note of the formula so you can remix if necessary.

Squeeze the colors into a saucer, add just enough mineral spirits to wet the color and dissolve it, and blend with a paintbrush. (For light color, add the dissolved tints to white oil-based paint – 10-20% paint to 80-90% glaze). Then spoon in a little transparent oil glaze, stir until color is evenly dispersed, and test on thick white paper. Bear in mind that the tone lightens when you add the rest of the glaze and mineral spirits, and appears less intense when brushed out sparingly on a wall.

When you're satisfied with the color mix it up with the remainder of the glaze in a paint pail; stir well. Test by brushing glaze very thinly over white paper and leave to dry – it looks softer as it dries.

2 Thin the glaze ▽
Use mineral spirits to dilute tinted glaze to a workable consistency. As the different glazes vary in thickness, start with 1 part mineral spirits to 2 parts glaze increasing the mineral spirits gradually (up to 2 parts), testing as you go. The more mineral spirits you add, the quicker the glaze dries.

Test the glaze *on a pre-painted board or a small area of wall (you can wipe it off with a rag dampened with mineral spirits). Keep the glaze to a thin film or it may run and apply quickly and lightly with a wide paintbrush.*

STIPPLING

Lifting off tiny flecks of wet glaze with a stippling brush gives a very finely speckled color: the effect is soft and unobtrusive.

1 *Apply the glaze*
Use an ordinary-width paintbrush to apply a thin film of glaze as evenly as possible.

Starting in one corner of the room, cover the wall from top to bottom with a strip of glaze about 12×24in. wide – whatever seems most manageable. Don't cover too large an area at one time or the paint will dry before you can stipple the surface.

2 *Stipple the glaze* △
Use a stippling brush or suitable soft-bristled brush held at right angles to the surface, to break up the color. Stab the tips of the bristles gently but firmly into the wet glaze – do not skid over the surface. Work over the strip of wet glaze leaving a narrow band on the outer edge unstippled.

Remove build-up of glaze from the brush frequently by brushing it out on paper. If necessary, wipe the bristles clean with mineral spirits.

3 *Repeat the technique*
Apply another strip of glaze so that it slightly overlaps with the first, then stipple the wet glaze as before.

Check the finish Stand back every so often to judge the effect. If you've left too much paint on some patches, try dabbing with the cleaned stippling brush. If the glaze is too dry to stipple, moisten the area with a rag dampened with mineral spirits then use a clean stippling brush.

RAGGING

Ragging creates a bold crushed velvet look. Rag-rolling (below) is similar but the effect is more directional.

1 *Prepare the rag*
Soak a lint-free rag in mineral spirits, squeeze out and dry by squeezing in a fresh rag. This prevents the rag from clogging up too quickly.

2 *Apply the glaze*
Starting in one corner of the room, brush on a thin even film of glaze to cover a strip of wall 12X 24in. wide from top to bottom. The glaze need not be brushed out absolutely smooth, but should cover the base color well so that the rag prints show up clearly.

3 *Rag the glaze* ▷
Bunch the rag up into a loose wad. Then press it lightly and quickly over the wet glaze, slightly overlapping the prints to get a distinct but soft, crinkled finish.
Keep changing the direction of your hand as you work and refold the rag every so often to avoid repetition. You can rinse the rag clean in mineral spirits, but change it for a fresh one when it gets clogged with glaze.

4 *Repeat the technique*
Brush glaze onto the next strip of wall, overlapping the first strip just a little so that you don't get a build-up of color along the join. Then, rag the wet glaze. Continue painting and ragging the wall a section at a time.
A second ragged color can be applied once the first coat has dried thoroughly (it takes about a week).

Check the finish Stand back every now and then to judge your work. If you've missed a patch, touch it up lightly with a glaze-wet rag. If there's a patch with too much glaze, rub off with a rag dampened with mineral spirits and immediately glaze and rag over again, blending it into the first glaze coat.

RAG-ROLLING

Apply the glaze in the same way as for ragging, but bunch the rag into a small sausage shape. Then lightly roll the rag up the wall (or down it, if that's easier) in an irregular, meandering line from bottom to top. One roll-up (or roll-down) should only just overlap with the next to prevent taking off too much glaze. Take care not to skid over the surface as you roll.

Leave a narrow band on the outer edge untouched to avoid brushing new glaze into an already ragged pattern. You can blend in the join when you rag-roll the next section. Replace rag with a new one as soon as it is saturated with glaze.

COLOR WASHING AND SHADING

Give your walls an added depth of color and a soft finish with one of these special paint effects.

Color washing and shading are the plainest paint techniques used by the professional decorator. They are relatively easy to apply (washing is easier than shading), giving broad brush effects that are very different from the more defined markings achieved by sponging or ragging.

Color washing has an informal cottage look. Use thinned latex paint over a latex base. The base coat should be white, or near white, with a darker color washed over it. For a more sophisticated finish, use satin paint for the base, and wash over an oil-based glaze to give more of a sheen. Again, the glaze is tinted to a darker shade than the base coat.

The technique in each case is the same: the wall is given a base coat of latex, and two thinned topcoats (of water-based paint over satin latex or oil-based paint over a flat oil-based paint) are brushed over randomly.

Color shading is a more precise technique. Bands of colored glaze are applied to a base coat and then carefully stippled to get a gently graduated effect. It's usual to start with the deepest color at the baseboard level and to finish with the palest tint or tone when you reach the ceiling, giving the room an open, airy feeling. However, you can reverse the process if you want to reduce the room's apparent height.

You can also give emphasis to the center of a wall by shading it from light in the center to darker shades at the edges. Color shading is also a popular technique for decorating paneled doors around the house, on cupboards and kitchen units.

CHOOSING COLORS

Because the aim of color washing is to create a mellow, 'distressed' or artificially worn effect, it's best to choose soft colors and pastels, giving an impression that stronger shades have been used and have faded. Think of apricot, aquamarine, apple green, butter yellow or old rose for walls – tones that reflect the gentle colors of nature.

Apply the top coat on a white base for a translucent effect, or over a paler version of the same color for richness.

If you are color shading you can use stronger colors, though it's wise not to have too wide a variation in tone or shade in a small room. If you are shading the walls in different tones of the same color, a look at the paint manufacturers' charts for specially mixed paints will give you some ideas. These ranges add different amounts of tint to a few base colors to produce related tones in different strengths. For color shading with two different shades, it is important to choose two colors that will blend together well – coffee to cream, blue to lilac and so on.

The gentle touch
Bring a softness to plain walls with a wash of apricot over a cream background. The added warmth gives a welcoming touch to an otherwise formal room. The nearly plain walls show off the fireplace and pictures perfectly.

PREPARATION

For any kind of painted finish, you should always prepare walls carefully – particularly if you intend to use a paint with a gloss finish that highlights every bump. However, one of the joys of a rustic technique like color washing is that the surface does not have to be totally flat.

Color shading requires more attention, and it is particularly important that your base coat is even, so that porous patches in your walls don't absorb the bands of tint unevenly, creating darker patches.

Always remove old wallcoverings before attempting either of these techniques, fill cracks and sand them level in the usual way (see Preparing Walls). Hang lining paper if necessary.

If you are redecorating walls finished with an oil-based finish, for example gloss, sand them lightly to provide a base for the next coat. Wash and rinse all painted walls.

If the walls are flaky, scrape flaking paint well. Finish with a coat of primer to get an evenly porous surface.

TOOLS AND EQUIPMENT

Color washing Besides paint, brushes and roller or pads for applying the base coat, the only tools and materials you will need are a wide wall paintbrush (4in.), a paint bucket and the glaze or wash itself. For matte color washing you will need latex paint thinned with water, and for an oil-based glaze you will need to mix the glaze from 50 percent oil-based paint, 20 percent mineral spirits and 30 percent oil glaze (see Special Effects with Paint). (For a more translucent finish, use a mix of 30 percent oil-based paint, 30 percent mineral spirits, 30 percent glaze and 10 percent matte finish clear varnish.)

Color shading For color shading, you need to mix several batches of paint (four or five), so use several paint buckets and empty jars to mix your glaze. The glaze should be made from 70 percent oil-based gloss, 20 percent oil-based paint, 10 percent mineral spirits. The tones or shades of paint are mixed first. To shade from dark to light, add increasing amounts of white oil-based paint.

You will also need a paint roller and tray for applying the shades, and a stippling brush to blur the edges.

MIXING A COLOR WASH

Using latex Tip some water-based paint into a paint pail and thin with water following the manufacturer's directions on the back of the can (the normal proportions are 1 part paint to 4 parts of water) and stir well.

Using a glaze Although the glaze used for color washing is thinner than the normal 'recipe' used for color shading and decorative paint techniques such as rag-rolling and stippling, the method used for making the glaze is the same – simply mix the paint and oil glaze, stir well with a clean stick then add the appropriate amount of mineral spirits to thin the glaze sufficiently and make it easy to work.

CHECK YOUR NEEDS

For the base coat:
- ☐ Paint for base coat (latex or a flat oil-based paint)
- ☐ Brush for cutting in
- ☐ Roller and paint tray
- ☐ Turpentine and warm water for cleaning brushes and rollers after using latex, or mineral spirits for cleaning after using oil-based paint or glaze

For color washing:
- ☐ A glaze of 50 percent flat oil-base, 20 percent mineral spirits and 30 percent oil glaze (for use on flat oil-based paint, see above)

OR
- ☐ Thinned latex paint (for use over a latex base)
- ☐ 4in. wall brush
- ☐ Paint bucket

For color shading:
- ☐ Several batches of glaze made up from 70 percent oil glaze, 20 percent flat, oil-based paint and 10 percent mineral spirits
- ☐ Empty jars to mix colors
- ☐ Paint buckets to mix glaze
- ☐ Roller and tray
- ☐ Stippling brush
- ☐ Mineral spirits and plenty of rags

COLOR WASHING ON WALLS

1 *Applying the base coat △*
Apply one or two base coats of white or lightly colored paint (you can use either latex or oil-based paint) leaving to dry between coats if you are applying more than one coat. Because the walls don't need to be perfectly evenly colored, one coat of paint should be sufficient. Work the paint carefully in all directions using diagonal strokes as shown.

2 *Applying the first wash △*
Dip the wall brush in the thinned latex or mixed glaze and paint the wall with random movements, working quickly to prevent drips and runs. If drips and runs start to form, work them in quickly before they begin to dry. Leave some of the background uncovered but take care to soften any hard lines. Leave paint to dry for four hours, glaze for at least 12 hours.

3 *Applying the second wash △*
Repeat the step over the previous wash to cover the base coat again. Leave to dry as before.

4 *Protective finish*
If you want a long-lasting surface, finish with a coat of matte or silk polyurethane varnish (add a dash of white paint to prevent yellowing).

MIXING COLORS FOR SHADING

1 Mixing the colors △
Start by mixing two shades of oil-based paint to give the desired number of shades. It's a good idea to use empty jam jars or coffee cans, so you can see the color clearly and check that they are thoroughly mixed. The four or five shades that you mix should be evenly graded. You can also use colored and flat white paint.

2 Mixing the glaze △
In the paint bucket, mix the oil glaze and mineral spirits, ensuring that all the mixtures are in exactly the same proportions. Then add the mixed paint to the glaze to give the mixture 70 percent oil glaze, 20 percent paint and 10 percent mineral spirits. Stir thoroughly to ensure all the ingredients are evenly mixed.

Note: The more mineral spirits you add the quicker the paint will dry, so stick to the 'recipe' as the bands of color will be more difficult to blend if the paint dries too quickly.

COLOR SHADING ON WALLS

1 Applying the base coat
Apply one or two coats of oil-based paint in the palest shade as a base coat, allowing plenty of time for the paint to dry (see manufacturer's instructions on side of can). It is essential to get an even finish, so in most cases both coats will be needed.

2 Mark the bands
Decide how wide the bands of color should be. The width depends on the height of the wall and the number of colors. For example, on an 8ft. wall, with four shading colors, each band will be 2ft. wide. Use a pencil to mark a very light line right across the wall between each of the bands of color, to give you a guide to the width of the bands when you come to apply the colors.

3 Applying the first band △
Tip the darkest batch of glaze into the base of the roller tray and paint a horizontal band right along the wall above the baseboard. (This is for walls shaded from dark to light, bottom to top. For other effects start with the darkest color at the top of the wall, or around the edges of the wall, as appropriate.)

4 Applying the next band △
Clean the roller and tray and tip the second color into the tray. Apply a second band above the first, so that the edges meet. Apply the colors in quick succession, so the first coat does not have a chance to dry out.

5 Softening the effect ◁
With the stippling brush, stipple up and down each band, 'pouncing' the brush softly up and down to produce the desired effect. Wipe the brush regularly using clean, lint-free rags, to prevent a build-up of glaze on the bristles. Stipple carefully over the join between the two bands of color to spread the color and blur the edge where the two bands meet. Then clean the stippling brush between bands, using mineral spirits or turpentine.

6 Repeat the technique
Apply the next band and repeat until you reach the ceiling. It is important to work quickly and be relaxed when you work to get as smooth and even a finish as possible. Remember you can always go over the wall again if you are not totally satisfied with the result.

METHOD OF WORKING

It is easier to achieve a good effect if you work with a partner, one applying the paint and the other using the stippling brush. The first person applies the first band of paint, and after applying a couple of yards of the second band of paint, the second person can start stippling to blend the two bands.

If you prefer to apply the base coat with a brush, it is worth having a separate brush for each bucket of paint so that you don't have to wash out the brushes between colors.

BRIGHT IDEA

Crafty art Highlight a picture by shading from a darker shade around the edge of the wall to a lighter shade around the picture. For a completely coordinated effect, use cardboard for the picture mount in a shade that exactly matches the darkest color used for shading. You can either paint the other walls in the darker shade, or repeat the shading effect on them. For this effect, it is best to use tones of one color (achieved by mixing different amounts of white into a color) rather than using two colors.

◁ *Successful shades*
Both the walls and the woodwork in this room have been shaded in tones of blue and green to give a gently graduated effect. The overall effect is emphasized by the use of neutral tones for curtains, sofa and accessories.

SPECKLED PAINT EFFECTS

Spattering and cissing are both ways of creating a speckled paint finish. Spattering is the easier of the two.

More defined than stippling, more delicate than sponging, spattering and cissing are two techniques that are superficially similar. Both employ tiny spots of color to produce a speckled look – the main difference is that cissing involves softening the effect with a solvent, and is best carried out on horizontal surfaces to avoid drips and runs.

Spattering requires little more than courage. No special brushes or paints are required (though you should use a specially made paint for spattering on china and glass and heat-set dyes for use on fabric). Nor do you need to have a fixed idea of the end result because spattering is one of the techniques that's best created in stages – simply choose your colors and step back to assess the result after applying each one.

What you do have to be careful to do is to mask the surrounding area thoroughly. If the piece is portable, spatter it in a workshop or garage, or outside on a mild day. You'll also need to take care not to overload the brush, which would produce splotches and streaks rather than spots.

Cissing, on the other hand, is a highly sophisticated technique. Unlike spattering, which is a random finish, it mimics the striations of natural stone. (It's also known as fossilizing because this is the look it's supposed to convey.) Purists keep pebbles and pieces of rock by them as they work so that they can reproduce the appearance but cissing can also be carried out in pastel colors for a fantasy effect. In cissing, mineral spirits are used to remove color and soften the design – a type of reverse spattering. Usually, a final, darker color is spattered over the surface to add extra definition. There are four main steps involved in creating this finish so it's not one to rush.

COLOR SENSE

Spattering looks particularly effective in contrasting colors, especially if these relate to the room scheme, and two shades of one color is a sophisticated alternative. It's often used to coordinate accessories like china, trays or cushions, combining two or three of the room's predominant colors, and generally looks best on a white or a pale toning ground. Think of peach and blue on a pale apricot or white, for example; pink and green on pistachio or primrose yellow and lavender on lemon. But dramatic color combinations like blue and purple on black, or orange on pink, can also look good.

Cissing is best done in softer colors. Blend the purple-pink of a crystalline rock like porphyry or the yellow-green of semi-precious stones like tourmaline or peridot with ivory and beige for a realistic effect and finish with polyurethane varnish, which brings out the colors like a rain-washed pebble.

All-over cover
Walls, woodwork and fireplace wall have all been spattered in tones of blue and white on a pale blue background. White ceramic ornaments and furnishings with simple lines complement rather than compete with the effect.

PREPARATION

Whatever the surface you are going to cover, it should be clean and smooth. Rub down glossy or oil-based surfaces with sandpaper to provide a base, and prime bare wood before applying the base coat. Old wood may need renovation before you can embark on a decorative paint technique. Strip away existing paint or varnish using a commercial stripper. Fill cracks with wood filler. Sand along the grain to a fine finish, by hand for small pieces or with an orbital sander for large flat areas. Seal any knots with knotting solution to prevent resin bleeding out and wipe the wood clean with mineral spirits.

Apply wood primer, then two base coats of a flat oil-based paint.

China and glass must be clean and grease-free so wash, rinse and dry, then wipe over with mineral spirits.

It is possible to spatter walls if you take care to achieve a fine spray of paint so that the spots won't run. In this case simply prepare the surface in the usual way. Remember that the wall will be speckled rather than covered with paint, so the base coat must be even.

TOOLS AND EQUIPMENT

Spattering Choose paint to suit the object you are spattering: latex for walls; enamel or commercial china paint for china and glass; gloss or enamel for metal and oil-based paint, latex, gloss or lacquer for wood. In addition you will need mineral spirits for thinning all the paints except latex, also for brush cleaning, and clear polyurethane varnish to give the spattering a protective finish.

Choose gloss or matte according to the effect you want to achieve. Paintbrushes required are a 4-6in. wall brush for large areas, a stiff artists' paintbrush for small items and a separate new brush for applying varnish. Last, you will need a straightedge or ruler on which to tap the brush when spattering.

Cissing The main requirement for cissing is the glaze. Make up three or four batches, using an equal mixture of scumble (oil glaze) and oil-based paint (see Special Effects with Paint). Choose colors that will blend together.

Paintbrushes required are two soft artists' brushes and a fine brush such as an eyeliner brush. In addition you will need a lint-free cloth with which to blend the first two or three glaze coats. You will also need a straightedge or ruler, mineral spirits, varnish and brush.

SPATTERING

1 *Apply the base coat*
After preparing the surface apply two base coats: gloss or semi-gloss paint on wood, latex on walls. Leave until dry (16 hours for oil-based paint, four hours for latex).

2 *Experiment with the paint*
Thin semi-gloss or gloss paint with mineral spirits and latex with water if necessary to obtain a good consistency. Experiment by spattering on newspaper until you are satisfied with the result.

3 *Apply the spatter ▷*
Dip the brush into the paint so that no more than one third of the bristle length is covered. Lift it a short distance over or next to the item to be spattered and tap the base of the handle on the straightedge to create a fine shower of paint. Continue until you have covered the piece and allow to dry completely.

Repeat the process (far right) using a second color and leave to dry again. Apply a third color if required.

4 *Varnish the spatter ▷*
When the spattering is completely dry, cover it with a protective layer of varnish. One coat is sufficient for decorative pieces, but use three on items subject to a lot of wear, such as table tops. Add a trace of white satin or gloss to the varnish to stop it from yellowing.

CHECK YOUR NEEDS

For spattering
- ☐ Oil- or water-based paint (to suit the surface)
- ☐ Mineral spirits if required
- ☐ Large or small paintbrush
- ☐ Straightedge or ruler
- ☐ Polyurethane varnish
- ☐ Varnish brush
- ☐ Old newspapers

For cissing
- ☐ Three or four batches of oil-based glaze
- ☐ Two artist's brushes
- ☐ Fine brush
- ☐ Lint-free cloth
- ☐ Paint thinner
- ☐ Straightedge
- ☐ Polyurethane varnish
- ☐ Varnish brush or new paintbrush

CISSING

Cissing involves dabbing two or three different glazes on a flat surface, merging the colors, spattering with mineral spirits and then spattering a final, darker colored glaze on the surface.

Here, we give instructions for a total of four different colored glazes.

1 Prepare the base
Apply two base coats of oil-based paint allowing each to dry thoroughly (about 16 hours for each coat).

2 Apply the glaze △
Dip the larger artist's brush into the first batch of glaze and dot paint at random over the surface. Clean the brush with mineral spirits and repeat the process with second and third batches of glaze while the first is still wet.

3 Blend the color ◁
Add a third color if you want to. Then, using the lint-free cloth, gently blend the three colors together just enough to create a mottled background.

4 Spatter with mineral spirits ▷
Dip the smaller (soft) brush into the mineral spirits and hold it over the still-wet mottled surface. Tap it sharply on the straightedge so that the mineral spirits spatters the surface. Wait a short while between each spatter, as the mineral spirits does not take effect instantly, and you can only see how much the color is being dispersed after a few seconds. Because the glaze is so slow drying, you can wipe over the surface and start again, if you are not satisfied.

5 Spatter with color ◁
Dip the same brush into the final batch of glaze and flick a fine spray of color over the surface by tapping the stock of the brush on a straightedge, as before or use a stiff brush, and run your fingers over the bristles.

6 Paint in the 'veins' ▷
Wet the fine brush with mineral spirits and paint in the 'veins' of the stone. Outline the veins in a darker color if you feel they are not clearly defined. Allow to dry thoroughly before coating with polyurethane varnish as for spattering.

BRIGHT IDEA

Spattering fabric You can spatter fabric to match your decor. Choose a light-colored natural fabric (such as a sheet or curtain lining) and use heat-setting fabric paint, watered down if necessary. Lay the fabric flat to spatter it. Experiment with different types of brushes: for example, try dipping a scrubbing brush in paint and running your fingers through it. Press underneath a piece of scrap fabric to set the dyes.

FLICKING

Flicking is a variation of spattering that combines streaks with spots. It is ideal for covering surfaces quickly. You can afford to load the brush more heavily and to be less precise.

1 *Prepare the surface* ◁
Start by painting the basecoat, then mask the areas that you don't want to paint. Thin the paint so that a streaky effect is created when it is flicked on the surface. Also use a slightly different technique: shake the brush with a flick of your wrist to achieve the desired freehand effect.

2 *Remove the protective paper* ▷
When paint is dry to the touch, remove the masking tape.

▽ *Stony look*
To imitate granite, this wooden box has been painted with a base coat of gray, and then cissed in pink and dark gray, and finally spattered with black.

MARBLED PAINT EFFECTS

Imitating the look of marble with paint is not difficult, as long as you limit yourself to small areas.

Marble has one of the most attractive natural finishes, and has long been admired by man. However, it does have disadvantages: it is heavy, expensive and cold to the touch. Perhaps it is for these reasons that painters have been imitating marble for thousands of years. When the work is done with real skill, it is almost impossible to distinguish a good fake from the real thing.

Such realism is beyond the capabilities of most amateurs, and many do not even attempt it. However, you do not need to be too ambitious. It is relatively easy to create the flowing, veined effect of marble without copying a particular piece of the stone.

Start by looking at as many examples of marble as possible, to give you a clear idea of the overall effect as well as the detailed colorings. It is often used for fascias on banks and offices, as well as fire surrounds and small pieces of furniture, such as washstands. Colors vary from creamy whites, rose, blue and golden marble to rich reds, greens and blacks. If you haven't got a suitable piece (such as a cheese board or pastry slab) it is worth photographing any unusual marbles that interest you. Magazines are another good source of inspiration.

SURFACES TO MARBLE

The technique described here can be used for walls, woodwork, floors, or furniture, but before you embark on a large project, practice on small items – picture frames, boxes, or lengths of molding for baseboards or architrave, for example. This gives you a chance to try out different colors and effects and mistakes on this scale are less disastrous than if you are working on a whole wall.

When working on larger items, remember that although you aren't going for a total trompe l'oeil effect, you should not defy nature. Only apply the technique to small areas – preferably surfaces that could conceivably have been constructed from stone. A table in a solid shape is a suitable choice: a chair with delicately turned legs is not. Marbleize wooden baseboards and fireplace mantels, but not doors or window frames.

Walls and floor can be marbled to great effect. Real marble usually comes in slabs, so it is a good idea to copy this effect on walls or floors. Divide walls into rectangular slabs and marble each one separately. Wood floors present the problem of how to cope with the boards: marble is never laid in planks. Even with the most careful filling the boards will probably still show. One answer is to cut plywood floor tiles and marble them individually, away from the site, before fitting them. Alternatively, lay large sheets of hardboard or squares of plywood on the floor before painting it. Varnish well to protect the work.

However adept you become at the technique, use it with restraint. Marbling the whole of a small room in a strong color can be oppressive: marbling just the dado, or fireplace and baseboard, will be much more effective.

VEINING

The veins in marble run diagonally. They spread out rather like a series of rivers with lots of tributaries. These tributaries do not, however, simply peter out: they must rejoin the main 'river' or cross or join up with another system. If you are unsure of how much veining to put in, always err on the side of too little rather than too much. A restrained effect is far more attractive than an over-busy mess.

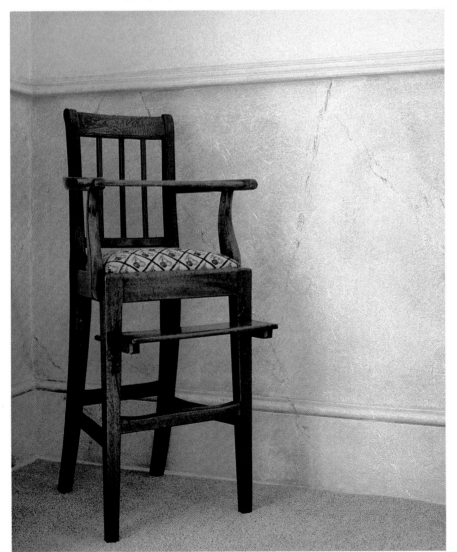

Marbled chair rail
Marbling the dado and baseboard softens the whole look of a room. It is a practical finish too, as it helps to disguise lumps and bumps.

33

SURFACE AND MATERIALS

The preparation of surfaces and materials needed for marbling are much the same as for other paint effects.

Preparation Prepare wood surfaces as described on pages 17-18. Rub the surface over lightly with sandpaper to give it a slightly rough base.

Walls should be prepared as described in Preparing Walls, pages 7-10 for basic preparation tasks and Hanging Wallcovering, pages 61-64.

The base coat is two coats of oil-based flat or satin paint. Brush strokes should not show, so rub down lightly with sandpaper after each coat to ensure a smooth surface.

The glaze is the same as that used for creating other paint effects (see instructions on page 22). Artists' oil colors or universal tints are used for dying the glaze, with white oil-based (gloss or semi-gloss) paint added for pale or opaque colors.

Varnishing not only protects the surface, it softens the veining effect and gives the surface the satiny sheen that real marble has. Use satin-finish varnish, applying two or three coats to woodwork and five to floors.

CHECK YOUR NEEDS
- ☐ Drop cloths/newspapers
- ☐ Masking tape
- ☐ Rags/paper towels
- ☐ Rubber gloves
- ☐ Mineral spirits
- ☐ Paintbrush cleaner
- ☐ Sandpaper

For the base coat:
- ☐ Oil-based paint
- ☐ Selection of brushes for walls, woodwork, or furniture, as required.

For the top coat and veins:
- ☐ Transparent oil-based glaze
- ☐ White plastic paint kettle (or old ceramic dish)
- ☐ Artists' oil colors or universal tints
- ☐ White oil-based paint for light or opaque colors
- ☐ Old saucer or bowl
- ☐ Old spoon
- ☐ Old paintbrush for mixing
- ☐ Scrap of paper for testing glaze
- ☐ Matte or silk varnish

For applying the paint:
- ☐ Paintbrushes
- ☐ Pieces of sponge
- ☐ Pieces of lint-free rag
- ☐ Fine, soft artist's brush
- ☐ Newspaper
- ☐ Feathers or soft paintbrush

WHITE MARBLE

This finish starts with a white or off-white base coat, which is left to dry. Successive subtly tinted glazes are added, followed by veining. All these must be done in one session: do not work on an area that takes more than about half an hour to cover.

1 *Apply the base coat*
Apply a base coat of white or off-white oil-based paint (you can tint white paint with artists' oil color to get the shade you want).

2 *Tint the glaze*
Mix up three gently graded tones of transparent pale gray glaze, using artists' oil paints or universal tints to dye the glaze. Thin the glaze with mineral spirits (about one part mineral spirits to two parts tinted glaze) to give a workable consistency.

3 *Apply the first coat* ▷
Paint a fine, even film of the palest glaze onto the surface. Use a bundle of rags to rag-roll the surface (see page 24).
This will lift off some of the gray glaze, leaving a very pale, two-tone surface. Leave to dry for about 1 hour, so that the surface is still very slightly tacky.

4 *The second coat* ◁
The second coat is 'ragged on' to the two-tone surface, to add further tones of gray. Dip a clean rag into the second batch of tinted glaze and wring it out. Bunch the rag into a loose bundle and press it lightly and quickly over the first coat. The preceding colors should still show through – you can leave quite large patches.

5 *Soften the effect* ▷
Immediately take a square of clean, dry rag about the size of a handkerchief, turn in the edges to form a smooth pad and pat it over the surface to soften the effect. Leave the surface to dry for about half an hour, so that it is slightly tacky.

6 Apply the third coat
Apply a coat of the third and darkest batch of glaze in the same way as the second. Soften as before and leave to dry for about 20-30 minutes (so it is still slightly tacky).

BRIGHT IDEA

Papering over the cracks If you don't feel you can tackle marbling yourself, but like the effect, use a marble-effect wallpaper instead to cover boxes or table tops. Prime the surface, cover with paper using wallpaper paste, then apply two or more coats of satin-finish varnish to protect the surface.

7 Add the veins ◁
Using artists' oil colors, mix up combinations of black, raw umber and white to give two tones of dark gray. Use a fine-pointed artist's brush to draw in the veins. Rotate the brush as you draw it across the surface to give you different thicknesses of line. (Professionals sometimes use the tip of a feather for very fine lines.) Paint in veins in both colors, bringing them close together at some points and creating a fine lattice in a single color in other areas.

8 Soften the veins ◁
Make up a pad of clean cloth as before and pat it over the veins to soften them and blend them into the background. (Again, some professionals prefer to use the side of a feather to do this.) Allow the surface to dry completely.

9 Check the effect
If the veins are too soft, add an extra black or dark gray outline to some of them for a more defined effect.

10 Varnish the marbling ▷
When you are happy with the effect and it is dry, apply two or three coats of satin-finish clear varnish. Allow to dry and rub down between coats.

BLACK MARBLE
This is a very dramatic finish that should be used with discretion. It is effective when used in smallish amounts to contrast with paler marbles – on baseboard and fireplace in a room with a rosy marble dado, for example, or as part of a pattern of marbled 'inlay.'

1 Apply the base coat
Prepare and prime the surface if necessary, then apply a coat of dark gray undercoat followed by one or two top coats of black oil-based paint.

2 Mix the glaze
This must be pale and opaque, so use a recipe of 1 part white oil-based paint to 3 parts glaze. Mix up with enough mineral spirits to give the consistency of cream (roughly 1-2 parts mineral spirits to 4 parts tinted glaze).

3 Apply the glaze ▷
Use a sponge or a fairly large brush to apply the glaze randomly over the background, leaving some of the background color showing through. You can leave quite large bands of black showing in some areas.

4 Breaking up the surface ◁
Scrunch up a sheet of newspaper and press it all over the surface to give a rag-rolled effect with a slightly veiny look. Change to a fresh sheet of newspaper when the first one becomes saturated with paint.

5 Softening the effect ▷
Take a square of clean, lint-free white cotton rag, turn in the corners to make a pad as before and pat it over the surface to soften it and merge the colors further. Allow to dry for about half an hour, so it is still slightly tacky.

6 Add the black veins ◁
Use a fairly fine, round artist's brush, or the end of a feather, to add a tracery of black veins, bordering and linking the darker background areas. Soften with a brush, cloth, or feather and allow to dry for about 15 minutes.

7 White veins ▷
Next add a tracery of white veins in the same way. They should run quite close to the black veins, and merge into them slightly. Marble of this type often has fairly large white areas, so paint in some diamond-shaped patches along the veins. A touch of green, added to the paint used for the veins, can look particularly effective.

8 Varnish the marbling
When you are completely happy with the effect, apply two or more coats of clear, satin finish varnish, rubbing down between each coat.

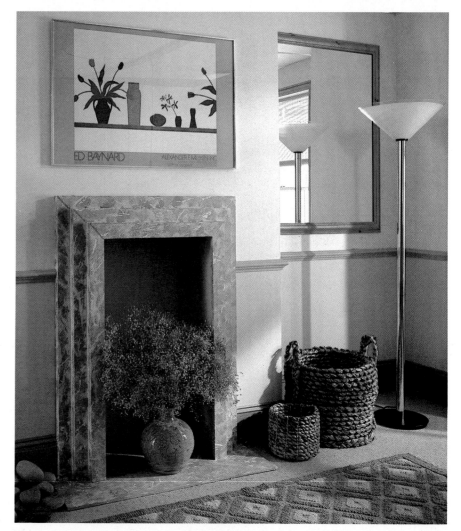

▷ Slate gray and smart
This faux fireplace has been given a simple wooden surround. The surround and a wooden 'hearth' have been marbled in slate-gray and black.

IMITATING TORTOISESHELL

The rich, almost translucent, tones of tortoiseshell can be achieved using traditional paint techniques.

Tortoiseshelling, like marbling, does not have to be a slavish copy of the real thing. It is, however, a good idea to look at examples of real tortoiseshell before you start work. The range of coloring occurring in the natural material is quite extensive – from two-tone blackish-brown and beige, to tawny gold and blond shades as well as quite red ones.

SURFACES TO PAINT
Flat or slightly curved surfaces are on the whole best for tortoiseshelling. This enables you to get a satisfying 'flow' to the pattern. You will also have a more realistic effect as real tortoiseshell could not have been used for exaggerated curves or intricately carved surfaces.

Real tortoiseshell was used in relatively small amounts, for inlay, on small panels, boxes, or the backs of hair brushes and mirrors. The fake finish, therefore, is usually used in the same way.

This is a lovely way to decorate a plain box, perhaps 'inlaying' the top in a blond tortoiseshell and using an auburn tortoiseshell for the border and on the sides. Picture and mirror frames, too, look sumptuous tortoiseshelled. Small, plain lamp tables can be treated in this way, or you could 'inlay' the top of a larger table. Tortoiseshell the frame or, better still, the panels of a door; not both. Take it off its hinges first as it is easier to work flat.

Tortoiseshell can also be combined with other finishes such as a plainish marble or simulated ivory.

You can, however, put realism aside and go for an over-the-top treatment. Choose a piece of junk furniture for this – an old dining table or wood-framed chair. This can make a stunning focal point in a room. Don't make the mistake of tortoiseshelling more than one such piece. A tortoiseshell dining table and simple black chairs can look stylishly unusual; a complete dining set plus sideboard will give you indigestion!

Creating the effect The tortoiseshell pattern should run diagonally across the work with bands of color diverging slightly. You should, therefore, always work in a diagonal direction when building up the pattern.

Isn't it rich?
Tones of dark oak, with the addition of earthy-colored oil paints are the main ingredients of this paint effect, imitating the look of tortoiseshell. Several coats of varnish create a deep, protective sheen, enhancing the effect.

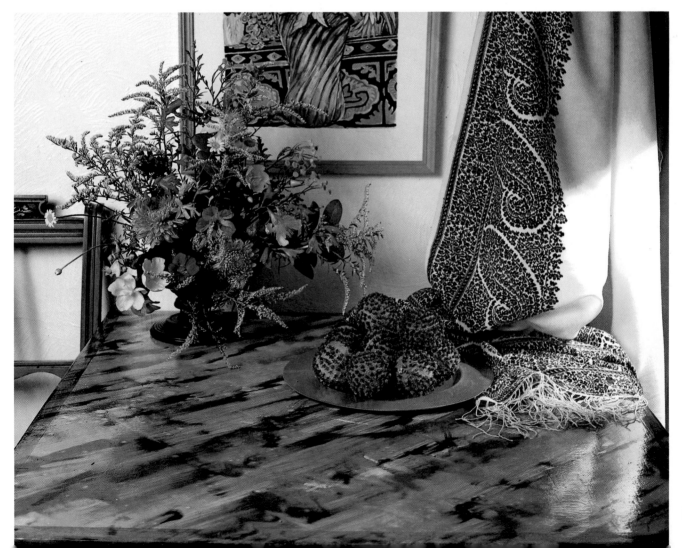

PAINTS AND VARNISHES

As long as you have gathered together all the materials you need, the actual task is not too difficult.

Paints Oil-based paint is used for the base coat and artists' oil colors for the tortoiseshell pattern. The colors used depend on the final coloring you want to achieve; the base coat is usually a strong chrome or acid yellow, with streaks of oil paint in dark tones; black, burnt umber, Indian red, gold, orange and so on.

Varnish This finish relies heavily on a very glossy appearance for its impact. There's no such thing as matte tortoiseshell. Colored varnish is the medium in which the effect is created and additional layers of clear gloss varnish give the essential glowing transparency. The varnish can be thinned with mineral spirits to help the colors 'flow.'

Varnish dries quickly so it is essential to work fast. For this reason, don't work on too large an area at once. If you intend to cover a large area, divide it into panels.

Work on alternate panels, leaving each to dry before tackling the ones in between.

PREPARATION

Prepare the surface carefully, filling any cracks and rubbing down thoroughly to get as smooth a surface as possible. Prime and then give the surface one or two coats of oil-based paint in the chosen color.

By varying the color of your base coat and using different shades of varnish and artists' oil colors you can create a spectrum of different tortoiseshells. Try out the effect on a sample board before starting work in earnest.

CHECK YOUR NEEDS

For the base coat
- ☐ Oil-based paint (yellow)
- ☐ Paintbrush of appropriate size

For the finish
- ☐ Medium oak and clear gloss varnish
- ☐ Mineral spirits
- ☐ Artists' oil color
- ☐ Paint pail for the varnish
- ☐ Saucers for the oil color
- ☐ 2×2-4in. wide paintbrushes
- ☐ 2×½in. wide artist's soft brushes
- ☐ Clean rags
- ☐ Plastic sheets/newspapers

CISSING

Horizontal surfaces can be cissed to 'open up' the color and give an interesting, antique effect.

Load an artist's brush with mineral spirits and tap it against a stick held over the wet surface of the work. It takes a few seconds for the effect to become noticeable so beware of becoming over-enthusiastic. Tap lightly, leave for half a minute, then repeat if necessary. (For further details, see Speckled Paint Effects pages 29-32.)

DARK GOLD TORTOISESHELL

The entire table in the picture was given the same dark gold tortoiseshell finish. When completely dry, and before varnishing with clear gloss varnish, the framework around the edge of the top of the table was given two coats of thinned dark oak varnish to 'hold' the center. The side panels and legs were darkened in the same way. Chrome yellow, oil-based paint was used for the base coat. You will also need medium oak varnish, black and burnt umber artists' oil paints.

1 **Apply the base coat**
Prepare the surface, prime and give it two coats of yellow oil-based paint. Leave to dry.

2 **Apply a coat of varnish ▷**
Thin the medium oak varnish with mineral spirits in the ratio of three parts varnish to one. Apply liberally to the surface.

3 **Break up the surface ◁**
Immediately tease the brush over the varnish to cover the surface with irregular diagonal zigzag bands. This creates an uneven background, imitating the irregular patches of natural tortoiseshell. Do not allow to dry.

4 Dab on darker colors ▷
Thin each of the artists' colors with a little mineral spirits. Then, still working in a diagonal direction, add squiggles of burnt umber to the wet surface. Then add blobs of black. You can also add touches of unthinned dark oak varnish.

5 Soften the effect ◁
Soften and blend the blobs of color into the varnish by stroking a clean, dry brush gently over the surface. Work in the same diagonal direction as before. Soften further by flicking the brush vertically, working even more lightly and gently. Then repeat the process diagonally once more.

6 Ciss the surface ▷
If you want to break up the pattern you can ciss the surface while it is still wet. Load a small, round artist's brush with mineral spirits and ciss very sparingly over the surface.

7 Soften the cissing ◁
Use the dry brush again to soften out any hard lines created by the cissing, working in a diagonal direction as before. You should now have a surface resembling tortoiseshell. If you are not happy with it, add further touches of oil color and soften as before.

8 Apply protective varnish ▷
When the work is completely dry, finish with several coats of clear gloss varnish. The more coats, the more luxurious and light-reflecting the final result will be.

△ *Tortoiseshell with a touch of red*

△ *Blue/green tortoiseshell technique*

△ *Crimson/oak tortoiseshell effect*

The method of creating dark gold tortoiseshell can be adapted to give a whole range of natural-colored tortoiseshells. All you need to do is to change the colors used for the base coat, varnish and squiggles.

Sample boards It is a good idea to try out different effects first – particularly when experimenting with fantasy colors – before starting work in earnest. Make a series of sample boards like the ones shown on the left and note the exact amounts of colors that you use, for further reference.

A pale tortoiseshell is achieved with light oak varnish and raw umber and yellow ochre artists' color over a pale yellow base coat. Dark oak varnish over bright sunshine yellow or brick red with raw umber and black artists' color will give richer, darker tortoiseshells. The sample at the top, on the left, is painted on a canary yellow base. A wash of medium oak varnish was used, with 'blobs and squiggles' of light red and burnt umber. The very bright yellow, coming through the rich oil colors, creates a warm, glowing effect.

Fantasy effects in addition, you can adapt the tortoiseshelling technique to give a whole range of fantasy effects.

Try tortoiseshelling over colors other than yellow – a bright mid-blue or emerald green. On these colors use medium or light oak varnish and black and a chestnut red mixed from vermilion and light red artists' oil colors. For an even more unusual effect, use one of the new colored varnishes, which are available in around 40 colors.

The two samples on the left are created as follows:

Blue/green sample Pale, gray-blue base coat, lime green polyurethane varnish, with Cerulean blue, Viridian green and Paynes gray oil colors.

Crimson/oak sample Warm, flesh-pink base coat, medium oak varnish, with Alazarin crimson, rose pink and flake white oil colors.

△ *Don't forget what the real thing looks like.*

BRIGHT IDEA

TORTOISESHELL FRAMES

Turn a wide, plain wooden picture frame into something unique and special by giving it the tortoiseshell treatment. This gives you an ideal opportunity to experiment and practice the technique. The darker colorings work particularly well on frames. You could make up a whole series of frames in different effects, including fantasy ones, instead of sample boards.

Similarly, experiment with other small items, such as wooden hairbrushes or small trays.

▷ *Traditional appeal*
A very traditional look demands attention to detail; color-washed walls, wood-grained doors and tortoiseshell-effect architraves and cornices, together with massed objets d'art create an extravagant confusion in this living room.

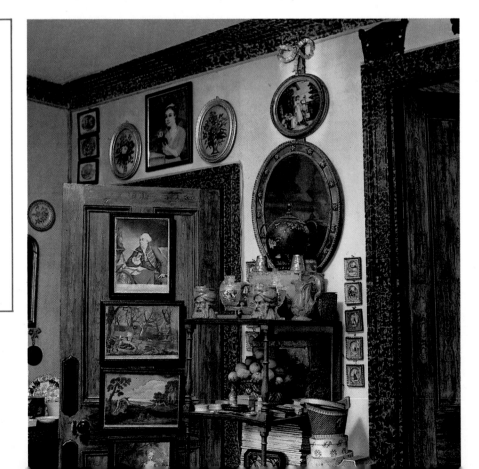

PAINT EFFECTS ON WOOD

Furniture and woodwork can be given a rich and original look by dragging or combing in attractive colors.

Most of the broken paint finishes that are applied to walls can be used with equal, if not greater, success on woodwork and furniture. Two paint techniques that are particularly suited to wood are dragging and combing. Both add an interesting depth and texture and are well worth the effort involved.

DRAGGING

This subtle, wood grain effect with finely graduated lines is made by drawing a long-bristled brush through wet glaze to reveal some of the paler base coat color underneath.

This is one of the most difficult paint effects to do well on a large surface as it requires a very steady hand. So, although it can produce some elegant results on walls, it's a good idea to master the technique first on smaller surfaces such as furniture and mirrors or picture frames.

Dragging also looks good on woodwork, especially when combined with other paint treatments on walls (such as sponging or ragging) but is too subtle to be effective on floors.

Proper dragging brushes, made of long and flexible bristles, are the easiest to use and give a very professional finish, but they are very expensive.

For woodwork and furniture, you can substitute a small oval varnish brush or ordinary paintbrush and get perfectly good results. A 4in. or 5in. paintbrush, a wide paperhanging brush or a painter's dusting brush, can also be used to drag walls.

COMBING

This is similar to dragging but bolder and coarser, and easier for a beginner to handle. In this case a hard comb-like object is raked through wet paint to make regular stripes or diagonals, or a pattern such as fan shapes or waves. The size and scale of the pattern is dictated by the size and spacing of the teeth and to a certain extent by the material of the comb.

The strong lines created by the comb make this an excellent technique for large painted areas such as floors. Perhaps because it lacks subtlety, combing is rarely used on furniture and woodwork, although it can be very effective if used with conviction.

The choice of tools for combing is wide. Ready-made steel and rubber combs are available in various shapes and sizes and are relatively cheap to buy. If they are hard to track down there are alternatives. A wide-toothed comb does the job well, or you can make your own comb from a suitably rigid material.

COLOR SCHEMES

To show up clearly, the dragged or combed color must be darker than the base color: either a deeper tone of the base color, or a color over white or cream. It's generally best to pick a stronger color than you think you need for the top coat as the final result is usually quite a bit paler.

Combed texture
Special steel combs are sometimes used to emphasize the grain of course-textured woods. Here, the tongue-and-groove paneling and baseboard are combed in deep blue over a paler blue that just shows through.

PREPARATION AND PAINTS

Prepare wood surfaces, priming bare wood where necessary. Then lightly rub down the surface with sandpaper before applying the base coat.

If you are going to drag the walls, prepare them in the usual way, hanging lining paper if the plasterboard is uneven or cracked.

The base coat for dragging or combing should be one or two coats of oil-based paint. Oil-based paint doesn't normally need undercoat, but bare wood must be primed.

The topcoat for dragging is the traditional transparent oil glaze that is tinted to the right color and diluted with mineral spirits until it is a workable consistency.

Glaze is also suitable for a combed surface. Or you can use an oil-based paint: either straight from the can or thinned with up to 25 percent mineral spirits but make sure that the paint is thick enough to cover the base coat properly.

Varnish After the paint finish has dried, it is advisable to protect it with several coats of clear matte or semi-gloss polyurethane varnish.

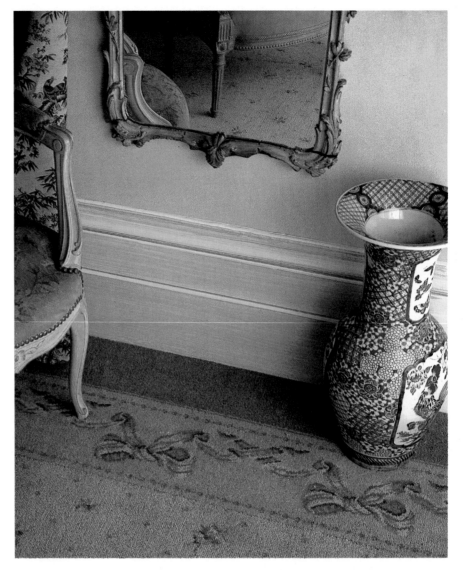

Dragged woodwork ▷
Dragging is an elegant finish that is particularly suited to formal rooms. Here, a delicate green glaze brushed over a pale background emphasizes the horizontal lines of the baseboard.

CHECK YOUR NEEDS
☐ Drop cloths/newspaper
☐ Masking tape
☐ Rags/paper towel
☐ Rubber gloves
☐ Mineral spirits
☐ Paintbrush cleaner/restorer

For the base coat:
☐ Primer and/or undercoat
☐ Oil-based paint
☐ 2-3in. paintbrush for woodwork/furniture; 4-8in. brush for floors/walls
☐ ¾in. cutting-in brush (for woodwork/furniture)

For the topcoat:
☐ Transparent oil glaze plus: white plastic paint bucket; universal tint/artists' oil color for dying glaze; white oil-based paint (for light colors); saucer or bowl; old spoon; narrow long-handled paintbrush for mixing; scrap paper for testing glaze
OR
☐ Oil-based paint

For the finish:
☐ Dragging brush (or 2-3in. varnish brush or ordinary paintbrush for woodwork; paperhanging brush or 4-5in. paintbrush for walls)
☐ Matte or semi-gloss polyurethane varnish for protecting the finish, and varnish brush
OR
☐ 2-4in. paintbrush for applying the topcoat
☐ Bought or homemade comb

▽ *Dragging brushes*

▽ *Steel combs*

▽ *Rubber combs*

DRAGGING WOODWORK

Taking off fine stripes of wet glaze to reveal a paler base coat creates a subtle textured finish that works well on woodwork and complements walls that are decorated with other paint finishes.

Brushwork The most important point to watch with dragging on wood is to follow the direction of the wood grain. So, baseboards, for example, and other horizontal pieces of woodwork are painted and dragged horizontally.

With doors, follow the normal sequence of painting (see page 20). If the door is paneled as on the right, brush vertically on vertical moldings and inset panels, the central and outer vertical sections, and on both sides of the door frame; brush horizontally on horizontal moldings and sections, and along top of frame. Work on one section at a time, and mask adjacent sections with masking tape.

1 *Apply the glaze*
Use a fairly narrow brush to apply a fine, even film of glaze in the direction of the wood grain. Don't try to cover too large an area at one time or the glaze dries before you can drag it.

2 *Drag the glaze*
Take a fairly narrow brush, and draw it through the wet glaze in the direction of the wood grain. After each stroke, wipe the brush clean on a rag or wastepaper.

Keep your strokes as straight and steady as possible. You'll find this easier to do if you hold the brush lightly and just skim the bristles over the wet surface – if you grip the brush tightly and press too hard, you can get wavy lines.

3 *Repeat the technique*
Stop dragging the first section of glaze just short of the wet edge. Then brush glaze onto the next section so that it overlaps just a little with the first, and continue dragging the wet glaze for a regular striped effect.

If you're painting a paneled door, allow each section to dry completely before repeating steps 1 and 2 on an adjacent section.

4 *Varnish*
Leave the dragged glaze until it is thoroughly dry. This usually takes at least two days. Then apply one or two coats of clear matte or semi-gloss polyurethane varnish to protect the decorative finish.

This is especially important on such things as wooden doors and cupboards, as they get a great deal of daily wear and tear.

BRIGHT IDEA

MARK UP A PANELED DOOR

For added visual interest, you can emphasize the structure of a paneled door by marking the joins or joints between horizontal and vertical sections after dragging, but before varnishing them.

Using a metal ruler and fairly blunt knife, lightly score a line along the joins between horizontal and vertical sections on the door. Then use a sharp lead pencil to fill in the scored lines, or apply a fine line of oil-based paint in a slightly darker tone than the dragged color. Emphasize the moldings by making the internal angles darker in the same way.

DRAGGING ON WALLS

The method for dragging walls is basically the same as for woodwork but, as the surface is very much larger, it really requires two people to do the job – one person to apply the glaze, the other to drag it before it dries. You also need to use wider brushes.

To help keep your dragged lines straight, use a plumb line and chalk to make vertical guidelines at intervals across the wall.

1 *Apply the glaze*
Starting in one corner of the room, use a wide paintbrush to apply a thin, even film of glaze in a 20-24in. wide strip from top to bottom of the wall.

2 *Drag the glaze*
Draw the dragging brush (or a suitable substitute) through the glaze from top to bottom of the wall, easing the pressure on the brush at the end of a stroke to prevent a build-up of glaze. Wipe off smudges with a rag dampened with mineral spirits.

If the wall is too high to drag in one easy movement, drag down from the ceiling to about waist level; then drag up from the baseboard, and feather the join. Stagger the joins to avoid a noticeable ripple across the wall.

COMBING

This is a bold finish that gives scope for some very dramatic effects, and it's a good idea to spend time experimenting with different combs. For example, you can create all sorts of effects by combing in first one direction, then crossing these lines with others. If you intend to do a lot of combing, it's worthwhile to make a sample book and record how different patterns are achieved.

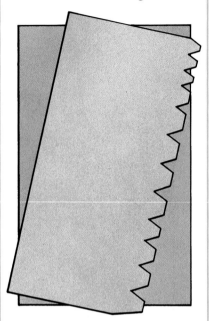

BRIGHT IDEA

Make your own comb by cutting V-shaped slots into a piece of hardboard, plastic or rubber flooring – or any similar semi-rigid material. A comb cut from a rubber window-cleaning

squeegee, for example, is particularly easy to use on floors because of its ready-made handle.

Cut several combs with teeth of various widths to alter the

scale of the pattern, making sure that teeth are spaced widely enough for the combing to show up. Try, too, cutting notched teeth of different widths on one comb for an interesting effect.

If you don't want to go to the trouble of making a comb, you could adapt a hair comb, or improvise with a simple item such as a tile adhesive spreader.

1 *Apply the paint or glaze*
Work in sections that can easily be combed while wet, and apply a fairly thick but even layer of paint or glaze, following the wood grain. If you're painting floorboards, start in the corner farthest from the door and work on a couple of boards at a time.

2 *Comb the paint or glaze* ▷
Draw the comb firmly through the wet paint or glaze to create a pattern of straight lines, waves, semi-circles or what you will.
Wipe the comb clean with a rag every so often. If you're covering a largish area, wrap a rag around the comb to soak up some of the displaced paint.

3 *Varnish*
Once the combing coat is dry, protect the finish with at least two coats of clear polyurethane varnish. Three coats of varnish provide better protection for floors.

PAINTING STRAIGHT LINES

Once you've got the knack of using a brush correctly, painting is child's play . . . until you come to the edges.

The only remotely difficult thing about painting is achieving a neat straight edge. For example, painting window frames and muntins is difficult enough to do neatly in itself. But the paint should extend onto the glass (both inside and out) just slightly to seal the junction between putty and glass so that condensation or rainwater cannot run down between the two and rot the frames. Getting a straightedge on the face of the glass is even harder to do freehand, especially if you are a beginner. The end result is often wobbly edges that simply look amateurish.

Similar problems arise when you're painting walls and ceilings a different color, painting baseboards, or if you want each side of a door to match the color scheme of the room it faces. Here you do at least have a sharp angle between the surfaces – an internal one between walls and ceilings or baseboards, an external one on door edges – but it can still be difficult to leave a straight paint line along it.

The last decorating area where you might want to paint neat straight lines is if you are being creative – for example by decorating walls or furniture with bands of contrasting color. Here even a steady hand may not be good enough to give good results. You need some help.

TOOLS AND MATERIALS

There are several tools that make painting straight lines easier, and one invaluable material.

Cutting-in brush Basically a slim paintbrush, this has bristles cut across at an angle instead of dead straight. It's mainly used for painting internal angles and you use it by drawing the edge of the brush with the longer bristles along the angle. However, this still takes a steady hand, so it is of limited use to the beginner.

Paint shield This is a metal or plastic plate that you hold so that its edge marks the line up to which you want to paint; at the same time it masks the surface you want to protect. It takes some practice to get good results as it is all too easy to get paint on the edge or underside of the shield and smear it where you don't want it.

The paint shield is most useful for jobs like painting baseboards, as it holds the carpet away from the board while you work.

Paint pad Designed for painting along

Band aid

Bands of white on plain Wedgwood blue walls form dramatic frames for the window, picture and vanity.

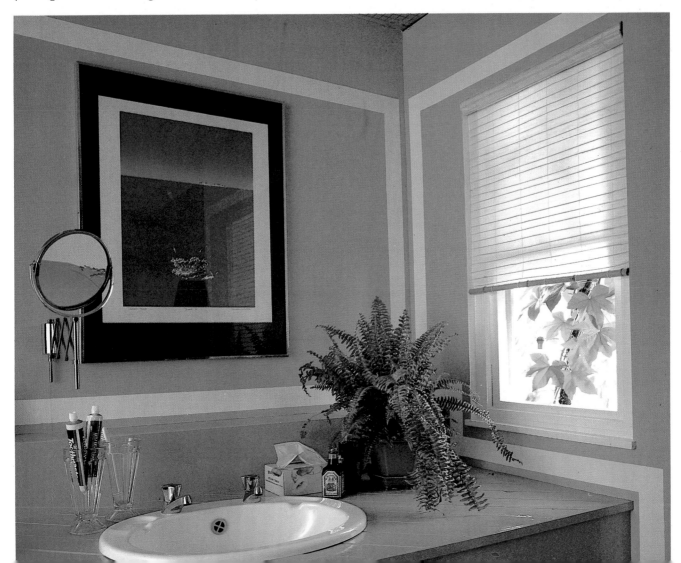

the angle between wall and ceiling or wall and baseboard, this has small guide wheels along one edge. You run these against the surface you're not painting, while the pad applies the paint to the one you are. The result is an edge that will be straight so long as the surface the wheels run against is true. If it isn't – which is often the case – the paint line will follow its contours and end up looking a little wavy.

Masking tape The most versatile aid of all for the sort of jobs described earlier is masking tape, a paper tape with a low-tack adhesive on the back used to mask any surfaces you don't want to paint. Stick it into position with one edge along the boundary line where one color finishes, then paint up to that line, allowing the paint to overlap onto

the tape. Peel the tape off carefully to leave a perfectly straight edge.

If you are painting with strong colors and want to butt a second color neatly up to the edge of the first, stick tape along the edge of the area you've just painted (when the paint's dry) and repeat the process.

To use masking tape successfully, first make sure that it's well pressed down onto the surface it's masking, or paint will tend to creep under the edge. Running over the tape with a seam roller before you start painting takes care of this. Second, don't leave the tape on too long, nor try to remove it too soon. Wait until the paint is touch-dry, and then peel it off by drawing the tape away from the painted area in a continuous motion.

Third, if you need to mask over a freshly painted surface, wait until the paint is hard-dry (overnight for gloss, four hours for latex) before you apply the tape. Otherwise, paint and tape may peel away together.

You can buy masking tape in a variety of widths; 2in. is generally the most useful. But if you are using a spray gun to paint sections of color, or painting a wall with a paint roller, which emits a fine spray of paint, use one of the wider tapes to protect the surrounding areas.

Dispenser Also on the market is a hand-held dispenser that applies a strip of brown paper to the surface you're masking, sticking it in place automatically with ordinary masking tape as you run the dispenser along the surface (see **Bright Idea**, page 48).

Cutting-in brush   Paint shield   Paint-pad   Masking tape and dispenser

CHECK YOUR NEEDS
- ☐ Painting equipment
- ☐ Cutting-in brush (optional)
- ☐ Masking tape, seam roller and sharp craft knife
- ☐ Paint shield OR
- ☐ Special paint pad with roller guides

MASKING WINDOWS
When applying the final coat to window frames make sure that the paint spreads slightly onto the glass. This ensures that the putty is completely sealed and waterproofed. Stick masking tape on the glass, set slightly away from the wood, to make it an easy job and obtain a perfect finish.

1 *Prepare the surface*
Start by washing down the paint job thoroughly, using a fungicide or diluted household bleach (1 part to 4 parts water) to kill mold spores. Sand with fine sandpaper, used wet, to provide a slightly rough base for the new paint. Rinse and leave to dry. Finally, clean the window panes.

2 *Stick the first piece of tape ▷*
Cut a strip of masking tape a fraction longer than the width of the pane and stick it to the glass parallel with the top edge, about ⅛in. from the angle. Press it down firmly by hand, and use your craft knife to cut the ends of the length so they finish ⅛in. in from the sides of the pane. Then peel back one end of the tape by 1½in.

4 *Finish taping ◁*
Finally, stick the fourth length in place and trim it as before. Then stick the peeled-back end of the first length over the stuck-down end of the final one. The reason for applying the tape in this sequence is that it makes it much easier to strip the tape off after you've finished painting – see Step 6.
Repeat the procedure for all the remaining panes.

3 *Add the next piece*
Apply the second length of tape to one of the side edges of the pane, overlapping it onto the stuck-down end of the first length. Press it down and trim as before.
Apply the third length along the bottom edge of the pane so that one end overlaps the end of the second length. Trim the end neatly as before.

5 *Paint the window frame*
Check that all the tape edges are firmly stuck to the glass. Then start painting, using either a narrow ordinary brush or a cutting-in brush. Tackle each masked edge first, then paint the rest of the muntin or frame next to it before moving on to the next section. Don't apply the paint too thickly, and brush it out well (unless using gel paint) or you'll get unsightly runs.

6 *Remove the tape* ▷
When you've finished, leave the paint until it's touch-dry (at least four hours for gloss, two for flat or satin oil-based paint). Then use the tip of your craft knife to lift the last end of the tape to be stuck down. Lift it carefully so you don't mar the still-soft paint. Once you have raised it enough, peel the tape away by pulling the end towards the center of the pane.

As you reach the corners, the overlaps you so carefully formed earlier will lift the next lengths cleanly away. Just change the angle of pull so you're always drawing the tape at an angle towards the center of the pane.

PAINTING DOORS

If you're painting the two sides of a door in different colors you'll be faced with two long edges where the color changes. This means you'll have to take particular care when painting them.

1 *Decide which colors to use* ▷
The convention is that you paint the opening edge of the door (nearest the handle) the same color as the face that opens into the room, and the hinged edge to match the other face. This ensures that when the door is open the visible edge and face match in each room.

Hinged edge

Opening edge

2 *Prepare the door*
Start by wedging the door open. Always unscrew all the door hardware – it's time-consuming and difficult to paint around it and you usually end up with paint on the handles however careful you are. Then clean the existing paint job. As for windows – wash down, sand lightly, rinse and allow to dry.

3 *Paint the edge of the door* ◁
There's no need to mask an external angle such as the edge of the door before you start painting; the sharp angle acts as a guide so long as you apply the paint correctly. Always draw the brush across the surface towards the edge where the paint changes color, using very little pressure as the bristles reach it. Then allow the bristles to run off the edge, and lay off the paint in the usual way with a final light brush stroke parallel with the edge. If you draw a loaded brush across the corner, you will 'scrape' a thick layer of paint off the bristles, and the result will be unsightly runs and a build-up of paint.

4 *Paint the face of the door*
Paint one edge of the door first, then its matching face. Wait until the first color is touch-dry before changing colors and painting the other face and edge (if this is necessary). Keep children and pets away until the paint is dry.

Then replace the door hardware, using new screws if the old ones are mangled. Leave the door wedged ajar at least overnight, otherwise the still-soft paint is likely to stick to the frame, ruining the finish.

PAINTING BASEBOARDS

If the walls are painted, rather than papered, it is a good idea to mask the wall when painting the baseboards. Also, if you have polished wood or vinyl floors or carpets that cannot be lifted, these should be protected.

1 *Mask the wall*
Mask the join between baseboards and walls by applying tape to the wall surface before you start painting. Of course, if you're painting them before hanging wallcoverings, masking won't be necessary; simply paint onto the wall surface by about ½in. so that any uneven trimming of the wallcovering won't leave bare plaster visible.

2 *Mask the floor*
Use masking tape along the angle between baseboard and floor if you have a 'hard' floorcovering – vinyl, woodblock and the like. If you have carpet, it's better to use a paint shield to hold the fibers away from the board as you paint it. Move it along as you complete each section. Strips of thin cardboard tucked under the baseboard will do just as well, and you can leave them in position until you've finished to prevent the fibers from getting stuck to the wet paint. Alternatively you can buy special carpet shields that you slip in and leave until the paint is dry.

PAINTING PATTERNS

Masking tape is the perfect ally for painting bands of color or creating geometric patterns on walls or furniture. Don't forget that the tape may lift freshly applied paint if you use it to apply second colors before the first are really hard. This means waiting overnight for gloss paint and at least four hours with water-based. Use chalk, a straightedge and a draftsman's square to transfer the patterns you want to the walls.

1 *Plan the pattern*
Plan out your design on paper first, unless it's very simple. It's best to use graph paper so you can scale the plan up to cover the actual surface you're decorating. For a simple band of color or a straightforward shape you can of course apply masking tape and work out the design directly on the wall.

2 *Transfer pattern to the wall △*
With a graph paper design, decide how many times you need to enlarge it and draw a grid on the wall. If the final pattern is to be ten times larger than the original drawn up on graph paper with ½in. squares, then each one will be 5in. square. Transfer the design to the wall one square at a time.

3 *Apply the first strips of tape △*
Next work out the order in which you will apply the bands and areas of color. Remember that you need to wait for one area to become thoroughly dry before applying masking tape over it and painting the adjoining area. Apply the first lot of masking tape, lining up its edge with the design, and start painting.

4 *Peel off the tape ▷*
When you've completed painting all the areas in the first color wait for the paint to become touch-dry and strip off the tape pulling it gently away from the freshly painted area. Unless you're working with water-based paint it's best to wait overnight before applying more tape over the fresh paint and carrying on with the design.

5 *Repeat the process*
Continue applying tape, painting, leaving the paint to dry and then peeling it off until you have completed the patterns. Remove any chalk marks.

▽ *Stunning stripes*
Short broad stripes wrapped around the edge of a chimney breast wall form a simple but most effective design.

BRIGHT IDEA

Spray painting Ordinary masking tape is fine for most painting jobs, but if you're using a spray gun for speed and quality of finish you really need a wider band of paper to stop the paint mist from getting where it shouldn't. You can do this by sticking strips of newspaper in position with masking tape, but it's difficult. The answer is a dispenser, which automatically applies a strip of brown paper (6 or 12in. wide) to the surface you want to mask and sticks it in place with masking tape as you move along the wall or door.

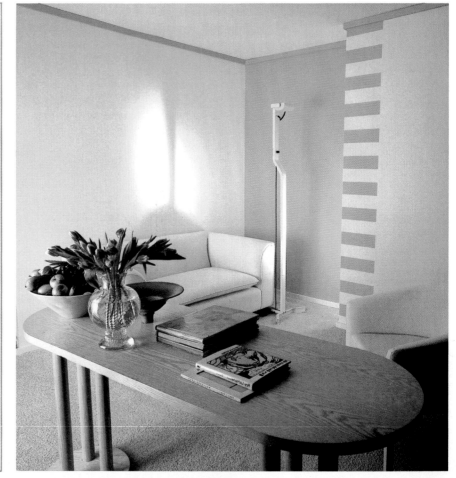

USING READY-MADE STENCILS

Stenciling is a simple and exciting way of adding color and pattern to furniture, walls, and even floors.

A stencil is essentially a decorative cutout through which paint is brushed onto the surface beneath. It can be used to add just as much or as little pattern as you like – a simple one-color border, for example, or a more intricate overall design in several colors. The real charm of stenciling is its simple hand-done look, so don't worry if you make an odd mistake.

Ready-made stencils are mostly available in simple folk style with lots of birds and floral motifs. You can also make your own stencils to complement existing furnishings.

Buying stencils Most stencils are made from stencil card or acetate sheet. Cardboard is strong and good for large designs: acetate is more expensive but it is transparent, which makes it much easier to position stencils accurately.

Some ready-made stencils are pre-cut, ready to use; uncut (ready-to-cut) stencils are cheaper but less convenient. They are available from specialist suppliers (often mail-order) and some art and craft shops.

The background Almost any surface will do as long as it's clean, sound and smooth: avoid irregular surfaces as paint tends to creep under the stencil.

If you're painting walls for stenciling, use water-based paint. Use a mid-sheen oil-based paint on wood; full gloss provides less of a base for the new paint.

Color schemes Try out alternatives on scrap paper first. Then paint a test stencil and fix it with masking tape to the surface you're stenciling to see if the effect really works.

PAINT AND BRUSHES

Paint The best paints for stenciling are water-based – they're fast drying so there is less risk of smudging and you can work faster.

Water-based acrylic colors are ideal and come in a wide color range – most art shops stock tubes of acrylics. Ordinary latex paint is almost as good. A 'test' pot should be sufficient for a small stenciling job or use any leftover paints that you have.

Flat oil-based paint is most suitable for stenciling on woodwork but takes longer to dry.

A stenciling brush, with stiff bristles cut squarely at the end, gives an attractive finish that is softly stippled. A good alternative is a blunt-ended hoghair artist's brush.

Both are available from most art and craft shops. Buy a brush for each stencil color: small brushes for small designs, bigger ones for large designs.

Clear polyurethane varnish is essential protection for stencils on wooden objects, furniture and floors. You'll need at least two coats of varnish on furniture and up to five coats on floors. A satin finish is suitable for most purposes.

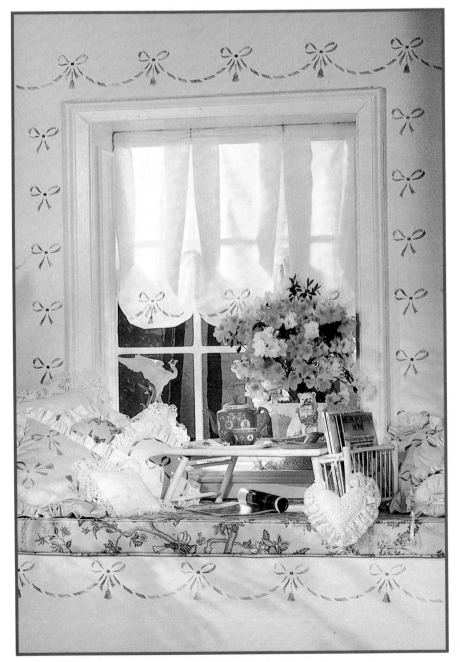

stencil brush

A coordinated look
A single motif in one color is used to decorate walls and soft furnishings.

Cutting out stencils △

Uncut stencils are supplied with areas marked for you to cut.

Fix the stencil securely to a cutting board with masking tape, then use a sharp knife or scalpel to cut out the areas to be painted. Cut out any small detailed sections first.

Take your time. To avoid jagged edges, always draw the knife towards yourself and keep going for the entire length of a cutting line. When cutting curves, turn the board rather than the knife for a smoother cut.

If the stencil is made of cardboard, finish off by smoothing down any rough edges with very fine sandpaper.

1 Prepare to paint △

If stencils are well spaced out, a saucerful of paint will probably be enough for the whole job.

Put a small amount of acrylic color or paint into the saucer. Whatever paint you use, it should be creamy, not watery – watery paint tends to seep under the stencil and smudge. If necessary, thin acrylic color with a little water and mix well with an old teaspoon; thin oil-based paint with a little mineral spirits.

2 Fix the first stencil △

Decide where you want the stencil and lightly pencil in the position; for marking out a border (see page 52).

Then smooth the stencil onto the surface, and fix in place with small strips of masking tape. When fixing on to paint or paper, remove some of the tape's stickiness by pressing it onto your forearm a few times.

Register marks If you're using stencil card and stenciling more than one color, lightly pencil around the top corners of the first stencil. You can then match the corners of subsequent stencils to these marks.

3 Paint the first color △

If you're using two or more colors, the rule is to stencil all of one color before going on to the next.

Dip just the end of the brush into the first color, and remove excess paint on scrap paper. Then dab paint onto the cutouts, working from the edges to the middle of each. To stop paint from seeping under the edges, gently press the stencil flat against the surface with your free hand – or with a wide-bladed knife if it's easier.

4 Remove the stencil

Leave the paint to dry for about a minute. Then carefully remove masking tape and lift the stencil off. Don't slide it or the wet paint will smudge.

5 Finish the first color

Complete the design in the first color. At regular intervals, wipe the stencil and the brush clean with tissue or a rag moistened with water (or mineral spirits for oil-based paint) to prevent a build-up of paint.

6 Paint the second color △

Let the first color dry completely, then start again with the next color.

Carefully position the second stencil. With acetate, align the printed register marks on the stencil with the painted design on the wall. With cardboard, match top corners of stencil with the pencil marks on the wall.

Tape stencil to the surface and, using a clean brush, apply paint as for the first stencil. Repeat this step if using more than two colors.

CHECK YOUR NEEDS
☐ Craft knife and spare blades
☐ Scalpel for intricate work
☐ Cutting board – e.g., scrap particleboard or plywood
☐ Masking tape

For painting the stencil:
☐ Paint
☐ Stencil brush for each color
☐ Old saucer and teaspoon
☐ Scrap paper
☐ Pencil and eraser
☐ Masking tape
☐ Mineral spirits (if you're using oil-based paint)
☐ Plenty of rags or paper towels

For marking out wall borders:
☐ Plumb line and bob (or any small weight and fine cord)
☐ Set square or T-square
☐ Ruler or straightedge
☐ Carpenter's level
☐ White chalk and pencil

Cleaning up
As soon as stenciling is completed, clean brushes and stencils. For cleaning off water-based paint, all you need is plenty of water. Remove oil-based paint with mineral spirits; wash brushes out in soapy water and rinse.

Gently wipe stencils clean with a rag or paper towel dipped in water or mineral spirits, taking care not to catch any fragile cutouts that might tear. Store stencils flat when dry, separated with sheets of tissue or waxed paper.

Finishing off
When stencil paint is dry, use an eraser to remove any pencil marks.

If you are protecting stencils with polyurethane varnish, allow two to four days for the paint to dry completely before applying several coats of varnish.

USING A STENCIL BRUSH
Don't overload the brush with paint: use it almost 'dry.' You can always make a stencil print darker, but it's difficult to lighten it once paint is applied.

Dip just the end of the brush into the paint, then stamp onto scrap paper to remove any excess paint. Holding the brush at right angles to the surface being painted, work from the edges of the cutout to the middle with a firm dabbing motion to reduce the risk of paint seeping under the edges of the stencil. Gradually build up soft translucent color leaving the middle of the cutouts a bit lighter than the edges to create shading.

STENCIL BORDERS

A stencil can be used to add decoration in exactly the same way as a wallpaper border.

For measuring and marking out a horizontal border design, follow the steps below. Be prepared, however, to make adjustments visually – few walls are absolutely even, and corners are rarely right angled.

1 *Mark a vertical line* ▷
Use a plumb line and pencil to mark a vertical line on the wall – just below the ceiling, or just above picture rail or baseboard level, depending on the position you want the border.

2 *Mark a horizontal line* ▷
Using the ceiling angle, chair rail or baseboard as a base, measure along the vertical line and mark with chalk or pencil the point where the top edge of the stencil will come. (If the border is to be at ceiling level, the top of the stencil should be slightly below the ceiling to allow for any deviation. If it's at baseboard or chair rail level, the bottom of the stencil should be slightly above the board or rail for the same reason.)

Position a set square or T-square at this point and mark off a horizontal guideline at right angles to the vertical line. Use a metal ruler to continue the line along the wall and right around the room.

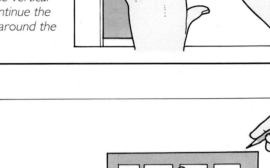

MARKING THE POSITION OF STENCILS

A regular motif pattern △
A regular motif looks best if it's spaced out evenly. Measure the length of each wall and divide by the length of the stencil to give you the number of complete motifs that will fit along each wall.

On graph paper, plan out how the stencil design fits the wall space, taking into account any spacing between motifs. Then mark the position of motifs along the horizontal guideline by penciling in the corners of each stencil – work out from the center of a wall in both directions to distribute the motifs evenly.

A continuous pattern △
With a continuous pattern, such as the greek key shown, lightly mark the first and last cutouts in the stencil onto the wall with pencil. Working clockwise around the room, move the stencil along to overlap the last outline on the wall with the first cutout in the stencil. Draw in the last stencil cutout and continue around the room.

If you're using two or more colors, you will also need to pencil in the corners of the first stencil as a register for subsequent stencils.

Turning a corner △
With a continuous pattern, you may need to take the stencil around corners. Score the stencil lightly along a straight edge with the back of a scalpel blade, then bend it over the straight edge to make a smooth fold.

Paint corner stencils last, but pencil in position of each one before continuing along the next wall.

BRIGHT IDEA

PAINTING A BORDER STENCIL
As you work along a border, make sure that you never place the stencil on top of wet paint. To avoid smudging the paint, do every second stencil and fill in the gaps later when the paint has completely dried.

MAKING YOUR OWN STENCILS

Designing your own stencil is an ideal way to add an individual decorative touch to a room.

Although there are dozens of ready-made stencils that you can buy, making your own gives you the opportunity to create a unique design that fits in perfectly with the style of a room. This chapter is a step-by-step guide to making a stencil. For painting stencils, see Using Ready-Made Stencils.

Design ideas You can draw your own designs freehand, or you can copy motifs from almost anywhere. Books, for example, provide illustrations of flowers, animals and children's story-book characters. Lettering is another attractive possibility, or you might 'borrow' a design you like from a wallcover-ing, fabric or embroidery.

Don't be too ambitious to begin with. It's the shape, rather than the detail, that creates the decorative impact, so choose a well-defined motif that can easily be adapted for stenciling in one or two colors. You can then get away with using one stencil plate, which is easier than using different stencils for different colors (see page 56).

Design and color sense Some designs may need to be enlarged for use, while very large designs need to be reduced. You can do this by dividing your traced design into a grid, then redrawing it to a suitable scale on squared graph paper (see overleaf). It may be easier, if you have access to a machine, to get a photocopy made to the size you want.

A balance of color is important in stenciling so try out alternative color schemes on scrap paper first. Then, to make sure the size of the design and your colors work, paint a test stencil on paper and attach with masking tape to the surface you're stenciling.

TOOLS AND EQUIPMENT

You will need stencil brushes and paints, preferably water-based. For making the stencil itself, you will also need the following:

Stencil material Traditional stencil card is like cardboard but has an oiled surface that doesn't soak up paint; it's strong, so it's good for intricate designs or very large stencils.

Acetate sheet is a little more expensive but has the advantage of transparency, which allows you to trace designs directly onto it as well as line up separate stencils for multi-colored designs. It is also slightly easier to cut, but requires careful handling as it is liable to split on sharp corners and curves.

Cardboard and acetate are available from most art and craft shops.

A fine-tipped felt pen to mark the design on stencil card; on acetate, use a permanent marker that will not smudge on plastic.

A cutting board – a piece of smooth chipboard or plywood makes a good flat surface for cutting on. If you're going to do a lot of stenciling, you can buy special cutting boards from art shops.

A sharp knife to cut the stencil – a craft knife is suitable, though a scalpel gives better control on detailed work. You will also need plenty of spare blades – a blunt knife can easily tear the stencil as you cut.

Dressing up
This white-painted dresser has been transformed with a stenciled pattern of summer garlands and fruit.

CHECK YOUR NEEDS

For copying the design
- ☐ Tracing paper
- ☐ Pencil
- ☐ Graph paper for enlarging/reducing

For making the stencil
- ☐ Stencil card
- ☐ Carbon paper
- ☐ Fine knitting needle
- ☐ Fine-tipped felt pen
OR
- ☐ Acetate sheet
- ☐ Fine-tipped permanent marker

For cutting the stencil
- ☐ Scrap of chipboard or plywood or a cutting board
- ☐ Craft knife and sharp blades
- ☐ Scalpel for intricate work
- ☐ Nail punch or knitting needle for punching out circles
- ☐ Fine-grade sandpaper to smooth edges of stencil card

For painting the stencil
- ☐ Paint
- ☐ Stencil brush for each color or small sponge
- ☐ Fine artist's brush for touching up
- ☐ Old saucer and teaspoon
- ☐ Scrap paper
- ☐ Pencil and eraser
- ☐ Masking tape
- ☐ Mineral spirits (if you're using oil-based paint)
- ☐ Plenty of rags or paper towels
- ☐ Polyurethane varnish and varnish brush (optional)

BRIGHT IDEA

Sponge it If you don't want to invest in a special stencil brush, cut up small pieces of sponge or foam and use them to dab on color instead.

Use one end of the sponge for one color, then let it dry and use the other end for a second color. Make sure that you don't overload it with paint.

ENLARGING AND REDUCING

If motifs taken from books or prints need to be enlarged or reduced, either use the method detailed below or have a photocopy made to the size required.

Trace the motif

First, trace the motif onto tracing paper as shown in Step 1, opposite.

Then, using a ruler, draw a frame closely around the traced motif and mark this area off into regular squares; an easy way of doing this is to stick the framed tracing onto graph paper (with glue or double-sided tape) so that you can use the squares as a guide. Last, carefully cut around the frame of the squared motif.

TO ENLARGE

1 Draw a diagonal △
Place the squared motif in the bottom left-hand corner of a large sheet of tracing paper – this must be at least as big as the finished stencil.

Draw a diagonal line from the bottom left-hand corner of the traced motif through the top right-hand corner, extending it across the sheet of tracing paper underneath.

Remove the tracing of the motif.

2 Draw a larger frame △
Decide how large you want the stencil to be and mark the desired height on the left-hand edge of the large sheet of tracing paper, X.

Draw a horizontal line from X to cut the diagonal line at Y. From Y, draw a vertical line down to the bottom edge at Z. You now have a scaled-up frame.

3 Copy the design △
Divide the new scaled-up frame into the same number of squares as the original small one. The squares will, of course, be proportionally larger.

Then carefully copy the motif, square by square, onto the scaled-up grid. It helps to first mark where the main lines of the motif intersect grid lines, then join the marks.

TO REDUCE

1 Draw a diagonal △
Stick the tracing of the motif over a piece of graph paper, draw a frame closely around the motif and cut out.

Place a small sheet of tracing paper – at least the size of the finished stencil – in the lower left-hand corner of the framed motif. Draw a diagonal line from the bottom left-hand corner to the top right-hand corner of the framed motif.

2 Draw a smaller frame
Decide on the new height of the design and mark the top right-hand corner of the smaller frame on the clean tracing paper at X. Join this point to the side and bottom edges of the small frame, Y and Z.

3 Copy the design
Divide this area into the same number of squares as the original motif. Then copy the motif square by square onto the scaled-down grid.

MAKING A STENCIL

If you are using acetate, and your chosen design does not need enlarging or reducing, you can trace the design directly onto the stencil material.

1 Trace the design
Place your chosen design on a flat surface and lay the tracing paper (or acetate) on top. If you're tracing from fabric, stretch the fabric out on card-board and attach with pins or tape first.

Then use a soft pencil (or permanent marker on acetate) to outline the parts of the design suitable for cutouts, making sure that the sections separating one cutout from another (the 'bridges') are wide enough to hold the stencil together.

2 Color code the tracing
If the design incorporates more than one color, color-code the tracing with pencils or crayons and keep it for reference when painting.

In any case, keep the tracing so that you can cut a fresh stencil if the first one gets damaged.

3 Transfer the tracing
Position the tracing on the cardboard or acetate to allow for a wide margin around the stencil design – see Step 6.

If motifs are to be repeated so close together that part of one is covered up as you stencil the next (e.g., a border), include the covered part of the design on the cardboard or acetate and use as a guide for lining up the stencils.

Stencil card △ Place tracing (right side up) over stencil card, with a sheet of carbon paper sandwiched in between, and fasten layers in place with tape.

Go over the outlines of the design with the tip of a fine knitting needle. Then remove tracing paper and carbon, and mark the design on the stencil card clearly with a fine felt-tip pen.

Acetate Fix the traced design (right side up) to a flat surface with masking tape. Lay a sheet of acetate directly over it, secure with tape, and draw the outline with a permanent marker pen.

4 Cut out stencil △
Practice cutting on a spare piece of cardboard/acetate before starting on the stencil itself.

Then place the drawn up stencil on the cutting board, and fix it in place with masking tape if you find this easier. Use a sharp knife or scalpel to cut out areas to be painted; use a nail punch or knitting needle to punch out small dots and circles.

Cut out small detailed sections first and larger areas last to avoid weakening the stencil.

Always draw the knife towards yourself, applying even pressure for the entire length of a line so that you get a clean edge. When cutting curves, turn the stencil material slowly around rather than the knife.

5 Tidy up the edges
When you've finished cutting, use the knife to carefully trim any jagged edges. Smooth down rough edges on stencil cardboard with fine sandpaper.

If you accidentally tear the stencil, repair it with clear, self-adhesive tape on both sides. Then trim away excess tape with a sharp knife, making sure that it doesn't overlap onto the edges of the cutout.

6 Cut stencil to size
Finally cut the cardboard/acetate to size leaving a frame of at least 1in. all the way around the design, otherwise the stencil will be weak and floppy.

7 Paint the stencil △
Tape the stencil to the wall with small strips of masking tape. (If you press the tape onto your forearm to get rid of some of the stickiness, it will be less likely to damage the wall decoration when you remove it.) Dip just the end of the stencil brush into the paint, removing any excess on scrap paper so that the brush is almost dry. Then dab paint onto the cutouts, working from the edges to the middle of each.

If you're using several colors, do all of one color before going on to the next. You can use masking tape to keep areas clean and separate: paint in one color, allow to dry, then change the masking tape without removing the stencil from the surface being painted.

8 Fill in detail
When you've filled in all the cut-out areas, leave the paint to dry for a minute, then carefully remove the tape and lift the stencil off. Don't slide it or the paint may smudge.

Use a small artist's brush to fill in any missed edges and give the finishing touches to the design.

9 Clean up
As soon as stenciling is completed, clean brushes out in the appropriate solvent: water for water-based paints, mineral spirits for oil-based paints.

Wipe stencils with a rag dipped in solvent and store flat when dry, separated with tissue or waxed paper.

MULTI-COLORED STENCILS

If a fairly complicated design is to be stenciled in several colors, it may be easier to cut a separate stencil for each color. In this case, you will need registration marks on the stencils so that you can line them up on top of each other during painting.

Color wise △
The carnation motif is stenciled in spring green and two shades of pink.

Borrowed style ▽
Inspiration can come from anywhere. Here, the carnation-ribbon theme was taken from the upholstery fabric, as were the soft colors. The large stenciled bow makes a pretty feature.

Acetate *As you trace the separate color areas onto different sheets of acetate, draw in a few dotted lines of other parts of the design so that you can check the exact position of each stencil in turn when it's time to paint.*

Stencil card *Trim tracing and cardboard sheets to same size before transferring the different parts of the design. Leave a margin around design for strength.*

Match up the corners of tracing and cardboard as you transfer the separate color areas to the different stencils. Before painting, pencil around top corners of first stencil; align subsequent stencils.

PAINTING MURALS

Add fun to a featureless room by painting the walls – with cartoon characters or a touch of realism.

Long before man had mastered making paper or canvas they drew on the nearest available surface – the wall. So murals were the first wall decoration and the first paintings. From these early drawings, artists developed and refined their techniques, so that in renaissance times some of the world's greatest works of art were murals. However, when it comes to painting your own murals, a sense of humor or of style is more important than technical skill.

TYPES OF ROOMS

Like any other dominant decoration, murals are best confined to rooms where they will retain their novelty value. The playroom or a child's bedroom, the bathroom and dining room are all obvious choices, and murals can also be used to transform gloomy walls and stairways and finished basements.

Consider any room without interesting features, particularly if it overlooks a dull view, but only paint a mural in rooms that are in constant use if you are confident it won't pall.

COLLECTING IDEAS

Before preparing the walls, you must decide on the finished effect and subject matter you want to paint. Decide whether you want a series of pictures to cover the whole wall, a funny detail, an architectural effect (such as a mock cornice or false fireplace) or wall to wall decoration. A term you may come across used to describe wall paintings is *trompe l'oeil* – a French phrase used to describe a picture that deceives the eye. Most trompe l'oeil effects do require a certain amount of skill, and involve more advanced paint techniques, such as marbling and wood graining.

A straightforward pictorial design is the easiest to achieve. The simplest have a picture book quality – one reason why murals are so suitable for children's rooms! Choose a theme that has large areas of flat color, like a Noah's ark, farm landscape, or seaside scene. Two-dimensional cartoon characters also translate easily onto walls – and you have the advantage of plenty of reference material to give you ideas. Look at illustrations in comics or books when you are planning the design.

For a more sophisticated effect, look at your own holiday photos: a view over tiled roof-tops, a haphazard Mediterranean village, or an exotic beach scene can all be effective. Cloud formations can be imitated on ceilings to create a restful effect in a bedroom or bathroom (where you are likely to spend some time looking at the ceiling).

If you want to create an amusing effect, there are some simple trompe l'oeil ideas you could try. Paint or stencil a vase of flowers above a shelf, or a pair of candlesticks and a clock above a mantelpiece. Brighten up a blank wall by painting a window with a view, or add potted plants, creepers and palms growing up from the baseboard, with birds and butterflies for extra realism.

Architectural details are a form of trompe l'oeil that requires a certain amount of skill. For inspiration, look at the wallpaper friezes available from smarter interior decorating shops, and at pictures of rooms with cornices, chair rails and so on. The two-dimensional representations will help to show you how to handle the lighter and darker colors to create a three-dimensional effect. You should also master some of the more advanced decorating techniques, such as marbling, before attempting to paint imitation fireplaces on your walls.

A repeat pattern, stenciled or painted freehand, though not strictly a mural provides wall-to-wall decoration with a rich, tapestry effect far removed from the regular, mass-produced and often slightly hard look of wallcovering.

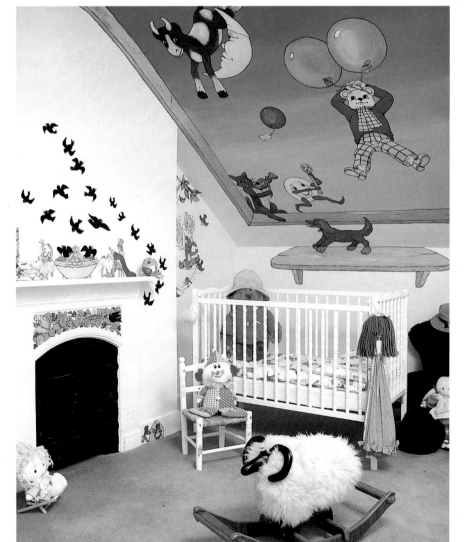

Add a smile
Children's rooms are an ideal place to practice your skills. Start with simple shapes, like the pie and 24 blackbirds, and if you are pleased with the result, go on to paint other nursery rhymes.

PREPARING THE SURFACE

Prepare the wall to suit the style of the design. Whatever the base surface you choose, the wall should be sound and fairly smooth, with no peeling paint or damaged wallboard. Most effects look best applied directly to the wall, rather than to lining paper. However, if the surface of the wall is poor, carefully hung lining paper, sealed with a thin coat of wallpaper paste before painting the base coat, creates a sound base.

A classical mural looks effective on a subtly shaded background that adds depth and richness. Traditionally, paints were not available in large quantities, accurately tinted by the manufacturer, so imitate the gentle effects of hand-mixed paint with one of the following techniques: apply a base coat of pale latex, with a slightly darker coat on top, sanded down finely to give the effect of a fresco (an Italian wall painting applied to wet plaster). For a translucent look, apply a coat of flat oil-base topped by a pale tinted oil-based glaze.

Stippled or sponged base coats also create background interest to the subject of your mural.

Landscape murals look particularly effective painted over a color-washed wall (see pages 25–28). Use color shading for sea or sky scenes.

Nursery murals in bright primary colors with clean outlines should be painted on smooth walls, with a base coat of silk or matte latex paint.

Surrounding walls that are not to be covered with the mural need to complement it, so it's a good idea to paint them to match the base on which the mural is painted.

Painting woodwork Mural techniques can be adapted to decorate furniture or doors. If you want to try out your skills first to see the effect, start by decorating a table or chest. The item should be primed, undercoated (two coats) and a base coat of oil-based gloss or flat paint applied before you start work. You will have to use oil-based paints on top of the base coat.

PAINT AND MATERIALS

The paints you use depend on the final effect you are after. Usually when painting murals you don't need large quantities of paint, but you do need a fairly large range of colors. In most cases it is best to use latex paint: you have to wait for one color to dry before applying the next, and latex is quicker drying than oil-based paints. (However, if the base coat is gloss or semi-gloss, you will have to use oil-based paints.) The problem is that latex comes in a limited range of rather soft colors, so you may need to mix your own colors.

You can color latex paint yourself, using tints, or economize by using small sample pots. Quick-drying artists' acrylic colors will give you a wider choice of colors, but these can be expensive used over a large area, and may be difficult to obliterate if you eventually want to paint over the design.

Equipment You will need graph paper to draw up the design, and chalk, a plumb line and pencils to transfer it to the wall. As well as the usual brushes for painting the base coat, you will need a wide selection of brushes for painting the design, including a tapered cutting-in brush for large areas, and artist's brushes and a lining fitch (a smaller version of a cutting-in brush) for details. Finally, you will need a new, fluff-free paintbrush for the protective coat of varnish.

CHECK YOUR NEEDS
- [ ] Paper and pencil
- [ ] Steel rule
- [ ] Paint for base coat
- [ ] Brush or roller
- [ ] Chalk
- [ ] String, plumb line and bob
- [ ] Selection of wall and artist's brushes
- [ ] Latex and artists' acrylic paints or oil-based paints
- [ ] Damp sponge
- [ ] Varnish and brush

Optional:
- [ ] Fine artist's brush and black paint
- [ ] Natural sponge
- [ ] Stenciling equipment

DRAWING UP THE MURAL

Pull together your ideas for the mural (pictures from books, photographs, postcards) before deciding exactly how it should look. Then measure the wall and sketch out a plan before drawing the mural.

1 *Choose your subject matter*
You probably have a fairly clear idea of what you want to paint, but it is advisable to collect lots of pictures together to give you examples of the details: a book of illustrated nursery rhymes for a child's bedroom, glossy magazines with traditional interiors for trompe l'oeil fireplaces, and so on.

2 *Paint the base coat*
When you have collected the ideas together, you can decide on a background color. It's a good idea to collect plenty of paint charts so as to check that you'll be able to get hold of the colored paints you need. Prepare the wall, filling cracks and sanding it smooth, and apply the base coat.

3 *Measure the wall*
Measure up the wall to be painted, and draw a plan of it. Sketch in the effect roughly on your plan: if you are copying directly from a picture or series of pictures, make sure they will fit the space you have, and decide where each picture should be positioned on the wall.

4 *Draw up a grid* ◁
Draw a grid over the picture you are copying or draw up the design on graph paper. The scale of the grid will depend on the amount you need to blow up the picture. If you are blowing up a postcard-size picture (3× 5in.) to go on a wall 8× 12ft., a ¼in. square grid is a good size.

5 *Mark the grid on the wall* ▷
Draw up a grid on the wall scaling up the squares to fit the space. In the example here, you should draw the lines 12in. apart. Use the plumb line and bob to get the lines straight, marking the wall with chalk, which can be wiped off easily. An easy way to mark the wall is to cover a length of string with chalk, pin it to the wall at each end of the line you want to mark, then snap it so the chalk marks the wall.

6 *Transfer your picture to the wall*
Look at each square of your original picture carefully, and copy it onto the corresponding space on the wall. Again, use chalk, which can be wiped off easily. Step back from the picture to check the overall effect, and smooth out any jerky lines. It is a good idea to complete your sketch a couple of days before you paint, so that you can come back to it and check the effect.

PAINTING SIMPLE SHAPES
Cartoon characters or a simplified landscape in areas of flat color are fairly straightforward to paint, once you have transferred the picture onto the wall.

1 *Choose the first color* ▷
Decide which color to paint first: it is a good idea to start with the larger areas. Starting at the top of the wall, paint all the areas that are to be that color. Allow to dry. It may help to put a tiny spot of color in each area before you start so that you don't miss one. If you need to mix different shades of the same color, start with the darkest shade, and gradually add more white.

2 *Add the next colors*
Continue in this way until the mural is complete, applying two coats to cover the grid marks where necessary, and allowing each color to dry before painting adjacent areas.

3 *Clean the wall*
When the paint is dry, wipe away what remains of the grid with a sponge.
When you are happy with the effect, varnish the wall to protect the painting. Use clear varnish with a dash of white oil-based paint – this helps to prevent the varnish from yellowing.

FINISHING TOUCHES

1 *Bold outlines* △
Use black paint to outline the characters, and give them greater definition. Outlining also helps to neaten any irregularities where areas of different colored paint meet.

2 *Adding eyelights* △
A dot or crescent of white paint in the middle of an eye will give extra life to the eye. Position the light patch so that it looks as though it is a reflection from the window in the room. (You can even paint 'window pane' highlights in the eyes.)

3 *A three-dimensional look* △
Make apples look round and characters look fat by creating shadows and highlights: mix darker and lighter tones of the color to be shaded, and sponge on the color to give a gently graded effect.

4 *Trompe l'oeil sky* △
Create a soft, summer sky by sponging clouds onto a pale blue background. Touches of pale salmon pink added to the edge of the clouds will imitate an evening sky.

BRIGHT IDEA

Even outlines A simple way to get bold outlines of images is to use a felt-tip pen: use a black marker that will not smudge. Test the effect of varnish over the lines before marking the wall, to ensure it will not run.

5 *Repeating images* △
If images are repeated on your design – simple flowers and leaves, birds or stars, for example – you can cut a stencil to make it easier to draw them. When using stencils in this way, don't just create the regular, border effect normally associated with stenciling: use the stencil as a template, drawing in the outline of each shape with chalk, and turning it to avoid regimented rows of shapes.

▽ *Undersea world*
Create a wet-look bathroom by painting the ceiling to look as though it is the surface of the sea. Add coral and a diving helmet – or just stick to simple goldfish.

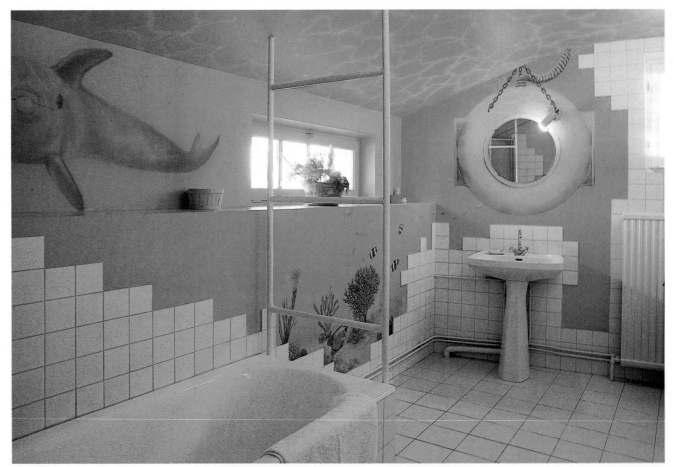

HANGING WALLCOVERINGS

If you are turning your decorating skills to wallcovering, be patient and methodical and you will get first-class results.

A wallcovering can transform a room with color and pattern and texture. It can also be the best solution for disguising less than perfect walls. So, if this is your first attempt at hanging wallcovering, here's how to do it step by step.

Preparation The surface to be decorated should be clean and as smooth as possible. Old wallcoverings are best removed and damaged wallboard repaired. For the basic preparation tasks, see Preparing Walls.

Seal new plaster with a thin coat of size – this will give the surface some 'slip,' making it easier to slide the paper into place, and will ensure a good bond. Sizing can be done several days in advance or about an hour before hanging the wallcovering.

Apply size (a watered-down adhesive) with an old paintbrush, and wipe off any drips as you go with a damp cloth (it is difficult to remove when dry).

Lining paper Plain lining paper can be used to improve uneven or cracked wallboard and provide a good clean surface for new wallcovering. It comes in various grades: as a guide, use a light grade under ordinary wallpaper and a heavier one for rough surfaces and textured wallcoverings. There is also a grade called Finished Extra White especially for painting over.

Choosing wallpaper Avoid cheap thin papers – they can stretch and tear easily when hanging. The best choice is a medium-weight covering, either plain, textured, or with a small random design (it is much more tricky to match up a large pattern). Textured 'relief' papers are useful for covering up bumpy walls.

This chapter covers the steps for hanging ordinary wallcovering that requires pasting. There are also ready-pasted papers. These are more expensive but less messy to use: lengths of paper are cut as for ordinary wallcoverings but they only need to be soaked in water for a few minutes before hanging.

TOOLS AND EQUIPMENT
For hanging ordinary wallcovering you will need the following:

A table for marking and pasting lengths of wallcovering. A fold-up pasting table is useful and quite cheap, but any table about 8ft. long can be used.

Size – a paste-like product for preparing bare walls. Although it can be bought, most wallpaper pastes can be diluted to make size following manufacturer's instructions.

Wallpaper paste usually comes as a powder for mixing with water. Any paste will do for ordinary paper: for vinyls and other washable wallcoverings use a paste containing a fungicide.

Plastic bucket for mixing paste (a wooden spoon or stick for blending).

A pasting brush for applying paste to the wallcovering – an old 4in. paintbrush is ideal.

A paperhanging brush with soft bristles to smooth the paper onto the wall. For washable papers, a dry sponge can be used instead.

A measuring tape for measuring wall height and lengths of wallcoverings – a retractable steel one is useful.

A plumb bob and line for hanging wallcovering vertically. Any small weight attached to cord will do.

Scissors – use long-bladed scissors for cutting lengths; short-bladed ones (or a craft knife) for trimming.

A seam roller to smooth the edges of lengths firmly to the wall. Do not use on embossed papers.

A sponge or plenty of rags for cleaning up any splotches of paste.

A stepladder tall enough to reach the top of the wall comfortably. Two stepladders and a plank are ideal.

For ready-pasted wallcoverings you will need a plastic trough to soak rolled-up lengths. A tube of latex glue is useful for finishing off any edges that come unstuck.

Share the load
The job of wallcovering is very much easier if there are two of you to share the workload. One person works at the pasting table, while the other hangs the wallcovering.

CHECK YOUR NEEDS

- ☐ Wallcovering
- ☐ Lining paper (if necessary)
- ☐ Paste
- ☐ Size (if necessary)
- ☐ Steel tape measure – and pencil
- ☐ Plumb line (or weight and cord)

- ☐ Table for laying out and pasting
- ☐ Long-bladed scissors for cutting lengths
- ☐ Small scissors or craft knife for trimming
- ☐ Plastic bucket

- ☐ Pasting brush (or 6-8in. paintbrush)
- ☐ Paperhanging brush (or sponge for washable papers)
- ☐ Sponge and old rags for cleaning
- ☐ Seam roller
- ☐ Two stepladders and plank

HOW MANY ROLLS DO YOU NEED?

Estimate rolls needed by measuring the height of the room from baseboard to cornice or ceiling and the distance around the walls. This chart is calculated for standard wallcovering that is sold in double rolls approximately 50-60 square feet.

Ceiling Height	Distance Around Room in Feet								
	20-27	28-33	34-40	41-47	48-54	55-60	61-67	68-74	75-81
8'	4	5	6	7	8	9	10	11	12
10'	5	6	7	9	10	11	12	14	15
12'	6	7	9	10	12	13	15	16	18

*Approximate number of double roll bolts per room.

NOTE: No allowance has been made for window and door openings. Number of bolts required may be less than chart indicates.

Buy all wallpaper at the same time, checking that batch numbers are the same to avoid color variations.
If the wallcovering has a large pattern, buy an extra roll.

1 *Plan your starting point △*
Start alongside the largest window and plan to work away from the light, so that if any edges do overlap they will not cast a shadow and won't be so obvious.

Large-patterned wallcoverings, however, should be centered on a main focal point such as a fireplace and subsequent lengths hung working outwards in both directions.

2 *Mark a vertical guide line △*
From the window frame measure out a distance of 1-2in. less than the width of your paper. Then use a plumb line and pencil to mark a vertical line down the length of the wall against which to hang the first length of wallcovering.

This will ensure that it is hung absolutely straight and allow for any deviation in the window frame edge.

3 *Measure for length*
Measure the vertical guide line, and add an extra 4in. to the measurement to allow for trimming the paper at top and bottom. (Use this measurement to cut all the full lengths of paper.)

Lay a length of wallcovering face up on the table and measure out the first length. If it has a distinctive pattern, always ensure that a full pattern repeat is at the top of the wall where it will be most obvious.

4 *Cut wallcovering to size*
Mark a cutting line in pencil across the wallcovering (check it is at right angles to the edges) and cut along it with long-bladed scissors.

5 *Match the pattern*
Before cutting subsequent lengths with a straight match pattern, match them with the first length. Pencil 'top' on the back to avoid hanging patterns upside down. Keep leftovers for short lengths – over doors, etc.

If the wallcovering has a drop pattern (on a diagonal), instead of a straight match, work from two rolls. If you cut alternate lengths from each roll – 1,3,5 from the first; 2,4,6 from the second, etc – the pattern should match more economically. Number as they are cut to keep them in order.

6 *Paste the wallcovering ▷*
Lay the first length face down on the table – with the top end of the paper aligned with the end of the table and the long edge fractionally overlapping the side of the table farthest from you. Start pasting from the center, working outwards and away from you to spread the paste evenly right up to the far edges.

Then move the wallcovering towards you so that it overlaps the front edge of the table and brush towards you to get a good covering of paste on all edges.

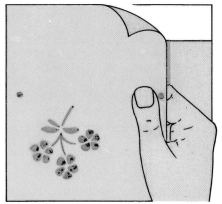

7 Fold the pasted section △
When the area of wallcovering on the table has been pasted, fold this neatly in half with pasted sides together. Move the folded section along the table so it hangs over the edge and paste the rest of the paper in the same way.

8 Lift the wallcovering △
When pasting is complete, fold the second half over, leaving a gap of about 2in. in the middle.

Some coverings must be left for a few minutes for the paste to soak in or they will wrinkle when hung – follow the instructions on the roll label. Lay this paper to one side and paste the next length in the meantime.

When the wallcovering is ready to be hung, drape it over your arm, as shown, to carry it to the wall.

9 Hang the wallcovering △
Use a stepladder to reach the top of the wall. Unfold the upper half of the wallcovering leaving the lower fold still in place. Do not let it drop suddenly or it may tear.

Holding the top of the wallcovering between fingers and thumb, position the top edge to overlap the ceiling or cornice by about 2in. Slide the wallcovering into position, aligning the right-hand edge with the vertical guide line on the wall.

10 Brush onto the wall △
Use the paperhanging brush (or sponge for washable types) to press the wallcovering against the wall – brush down the center, then firmly out towards the edges. If it bubbles or wrinkles, gently peel it away to release the air and brush back into place. Unfold the lower half and brush out in the same way.

11 Trim the edges △
Press the top edge into the angle of wall and ceiling or cornice with the back of a scissors' blade. Peel back the wallcovering, cut along the crease, and use the tip of the hanging brush to dab the end neatly back into place. If

necessary, add a little extra paste to the top edge first.

Trim the edge at baseboard level in the same way, and along the window frame if it overlaps.

Remove any paste from the ceiling or woodwork with a damp sponge.

12 Hang the second length ▷
Hang the second length in the same way, butting the edges together. Match the pattern if there is one by sliding the paper up or down using the palms of your hands. Brush into place and trim as before.

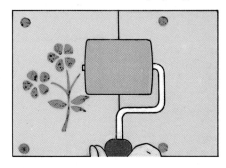

13 Use a seam roller △
To smooth the edges, go over the seams with a seam roller about 20 minutes after hanging. Do not roll embossed papers – dab seams firmly with the hanging brush instead.

Turning a corner ▷

Room corners are rarely square, so a length of wallcovering that turns a corner should be hung as two strips. Measure the distance from the last length to the corner in several places. For internal corners, add ½in. to the widest measurement; for external corners, such as around a chimney breast, add 1½in.

Cut a length of wallcovering to this width and hang it with the cut edge brushed into (or around) the corner. Measure the width of the remainder and then measure this distance from the corner. Hang a plumb line from this point and mark the wall. Paste and hang the wallcovering, overlapping the amount carried around – any slight pattern mismatch will not show.

Paper a window recess △

Paper the inside of the recess first, turning a ½in. flap onto the surrounding wall. Then paper the wall around the window, cutting out the shape exactly.

radiator bracket

Work around doors and windows △

Hang the length in the normal way, but allow it to hang over the face of the closed door. Trim wallcovering roughly to the shape of the frame, allowing about 1in. overlap, and make a ½in. diagonal cut into corner.

Brush the wallcovering into the angle between wall and frame, mark a crease line with the back of the scissors and trim.

If possible, center short lengths over doors and windows with full lengths on either side.

Work around switches and outlets △

Paper over a light switch or outlet, then use a sharp knife to make diagonal cuts to the corners (or several cuts if it is circular). Press the flaps back into position and trim the edges.

If the face plate is removable, turn off the electricity at the main switch and then unscrew the plate. Instead of trimming off the flaps, simply tuck them behind the plate. Do not use this method with foil wallcoverings.

Work around radiators △

Let the wallcovering hang over the face of the radiator and cut a slit up from the bottom of the length so that it can pass either side of the radiator bracket. Then make ½in. horizontal slits at top and bottom of bracket. Tuck wallcovering behind radiator and smooth around the bracket fixture.

BRIGHT IDEA

A NEAT EDGE

After decorating, hang a wallcovering border at ceiling level to tidy up edges. If a cornice ends with a sloping ceiling (in a stairwell, say) trim the border edge and paste it over the short end to highlight the angle.

LINING PAPER

If lining paper is to be painted over, hang it vertically as for standard wallpaper.

If it is to be covered with another wallcovering, hang it horizontally to avoid vertical joins coinciding in the two layers. Use the same paste that will be used for the final wallcovering.

Start at ceiling level and work down, butting joins closely. Leave to dry for 24 hours. If edges do overlap, lightly rub them down with medium-grade sandpaper.

DECORATING CEILINGS

Covering a ceiling can give a room an attractive new look as well as hide fine cracks and uneven plaster.

Although covering a ceiling is not the easiest of jobs, there are far fewer obstructions to cope with than you'll find when papering the walls of a typical room. It is still, however, best tackled by two people – with one person supporting the weight of the paper while the other coaxes it into position. If you are covering a whole room, start with the ceiling and then do the walls. If you are also putting up a ceiling rose (page 68), fix the rose after rather than before the walls are covered.

Choosing wallcovering Steer clear of cheap, thin wallcovering that can stretch and tear easily when wet with paste.

Choose a medium-weight wallcovering, either plain or with a small design so that you don't have to worry about matching it up.

If the ceiling is in poor condition but you want a painted finish, a fine-textured paper is a good choice. Heavier relief and embossed papers are difficult to handle at ceiling height.

Preparation Prepare a ceiling for decorating as you would wallboard but don't worry about hairline cracks that will be hidden by the wallcovering. If the ceiling is newly plastered, treat it with a generous coat of size (watered-down wallpaper paste).

Before you start to work on the ceiling, remove any light fixtures.

Where to start It's traditional to work inwards from and parallel to the main window in the room so that any overlapping edges won't be highlighted. However, it may be easier to work at right angles to the window if this means that you'll be handling shorter, more manageable lengths of paper (in a long, thin room for example).

TOOLS AND EQUIPMENT

You need the same tool kit for covering a ceiling as you do for basic wallcovering (see Hanging Wallcovering, pages 61-64).

You may also need a screwdriver to take down ceiling lights: it's easier to do this than try to work around them.

Access For safety and comfort, you need a strong platform that can be positioned at working height directly beneath each length. It's no good trying to perch on chairs or small steps.

All-over print
Pretty coordinating paper on the ceiling creates a cozy and intimate bedroom.

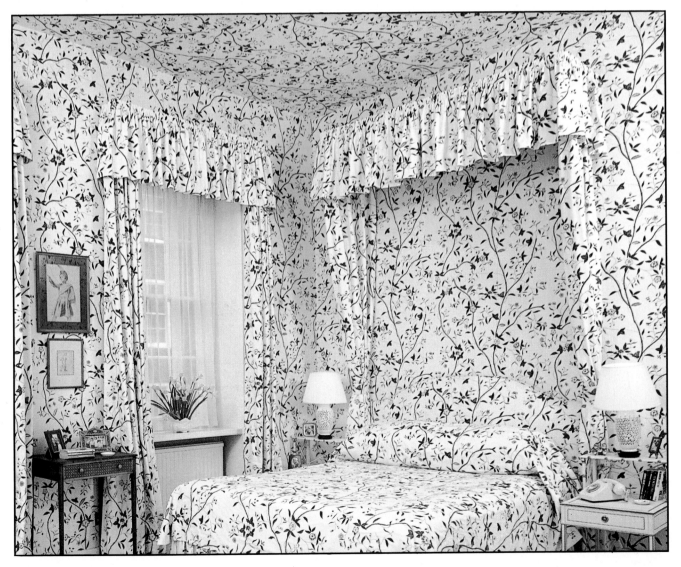

CHECK YOUR NEEDS
☐ Wallcovering
☐ Paste
☐ Steel tape and pencil
☐ String and colored chalk
☐ Table for cutting and pasting
☐ Long-bladed scissors
☐ Small scissors or craft knife
☐ Plastic bucket for paste
☐ Pasting brush or 8in. paint-
  brush
☐ Paperhanging brush (or sponge
  for washables)
☐ Screwdriver
☐ Old rags or sponge
☐ Seam roller
☐ Stepladders, planks, etc.

HOW MANY ROLLS?
Estimate the number of rolls you need by measuring the distance around the walls of the room.
This chart is calculated for standard wallpaper that is sold in double roll bolts approximately 50-60 sq.ft.

Distance around the room (ft.)	33	36	40	43	46	50	53	56	60	63	66
No. of double rolls		2	2	2	3	3	4	4	4	5	5	5

Distance around the room (ft.)	70	73	76	80	83	86	90	93	96	99
No. of double rolls	6	7	7	8	8	9	10	10	11	11

Buy all wallcovering at the same time, checking that batch numbers are the same to avoid color variations. If the wallcovering has a pattern, buy an extra roll.

1 Mark a guideline ▷
Decide where you're going to start.
Then, at both ends of the wall you'll be working from, measure out across the ceiling a distance of 1-2in. less than the width of the wallcovering to allow an overlap at the wall angle; mark with a pencil.
Coat a length of string with colored chalk. Pin to the ceiling edges, aligned with the pencil marks, and snap it against the ceiling. Remove string.

2 Cut covering to size
Measure from wall to wall and cut the first length, allowing an extra 4in. for trimming the wallcovering at each end.
Cut all the other lengths too. If the wallcovering has a pattern, match subsequent lengths with the previous one. Number and mark the backs so that it is hung in the right order and the pattern is always in the same direction.

3 Paste and fold △
Mix up the adhesive according to manufacturer's instructions. Then lay the first length face down on the table and paste in the normal way but fold in a concertina fashion: paste an area almost as long as the table and fold this up into a series of pleats about 18in. wide, keeping the pasted side inside each fold.
Move the folded wallcovering along the table, and paste and fold the rest of it in the same way. When you reach the far end of the length, turn the last fold back on itself to ensure that you don't get paste on the front of the wallcovering.

4 Paste the ceiling ▷
Some wallcoverings must be left for a few minutes for the paste to soak in or they'll wrinkle when hung – follow the instructions on the roll label. Lay this wallcovering to one side and paste the next length in the meantime.
When you're ready to hang the wallcovering, apply some adhesive to the ceiling itself at the start of each length so that the covering won't come unstuck as you work along the ceiling.

5 Hang the first length ▷

If you are working on your own, carefully pick up the pasted wallcovering, using a roll of wallcovering to support it in one hand while you brush it into place with the other.

To hang the first length, start in one corner, facing the wall you are working from. Peel back the last fold you made, line it up with the chalk line and brush the wallcovering firmly into the angles between wall and ceiling. Remember to leave enough for trimming.

Moving back along the work platform, gradually unfold the wallcovering and brush out to remove any air bubbles. Make sure you hold the folded length as close to the ceiling as possible – this can be tiring but if you let your arm drop, the weight of the folds may drag the newly pasted covering away from the ceiling.

Working in pairs ▷

If you have a helper, one person can support the wallcovering on a clean broom from floor-level while the other walks along the platform brushing it onto the ceiling. This makes the job much easier, and is far less tiring. Hang the covering in the same way as described above.

6 Trim the edges ▷

At short and long side edges, trim the covering so that it butts neatly up to wall or molding. If there is no molding or you will cover the walls next, allow a ½in. overlap.

To trim, crease covering into ceiling angle with the back of a scissor blade. Peel it back, cut along crease, and brush back down. Finish by wiping off any smears of paste with a damp rag or sponge.

7 Hang the other lengths

Working away from the wall, hang subsequent lengths in exactly the same way as the first. Butt the edges neatly together, and match the pattern if any.

The last length will probably be less than a full width. Measure and cut to size before pasting and hanging, allowing 2in. extra width for trimming the long side edge against the wall.

8 Use a seam roller

When all the lengths are hung, go over the seams with a seam roller to make sure that the edges of each length are well stuck down. Place a piece of paper under the roller so that it doesn't mark the newly pasted wallcovering.

Do not roll relief or embossed papers – dab the seams firmly with the ends of the hanging brush or a soft cloth instead.

CUTTING AROUND FIXTURES

Before starting to cover the ceiling, **turn off the electricity at the main switch.** The main fuse box is usually found in an out of the way closet or corner of the kitchen or hall; the main switch will read OFF in large letters when the power is turned off.

Then remove light bulb and shade, unscrew the cover and disconnect the wire (make a color drawing of the wiring first so that you can replace it correctly). To protect the wiring from wet paste, screw the cover back on before covering over it.

1 Pierce the covering

Paper the ceiling as described above up to the light position. When you come to the cover, press the wallcovering lightly over it. Then pierce the covering directly beneath the light cover with a sharp pair of scissors.

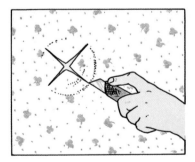

2 Cut and trim △

Make several cuts outwards from the hole to reveal the cover. Partly unscrew the cover, brush the wallcovering around it and trim until there is just enough left to tuck behind. Press the edges of the wallcovering firmly onto the ceiling, then continue hanging the rest of the length. Finish by replacing the wire and light cover.

BRIGHT IDEA

CUT OUT AIR BUBBLES

Use a sharp knife or razor blade to cut a neat cross in any bubbles that are still there a couple of days after covering.

Fold back the corners of the cuts, dab some paste behind, then smooth the flaps back and press firmly into position. Wipe off any excess paste with a damp sponge or rag.

DECORATIVE CEILING ROSES

A ceiling rose is a flat, circular center-piece, often used with a suspended light fixture. The steps below cover installing a rose with a back recess to cover electrical connections.

Buying a ceiling rose Ceiling roses come in a wide range of sizes and designs. Most are made from traditional fiberous plaster or from less expensive materials such as polystyrene and polyurethane. Plaster types are heavy: they must be nailed or screwed to the joists above the ceiling as well as stuck into position. Plastic types are light and can be glued to the ceiling, although it's best to use panel pins as well for extra support. Always use adhesive and fixtures that are recommended by the manufacturer.

1 *Find the room center*
Except in long rooms where two roses may be fitted, it's usual to fit the rose in the center of the ceiling. If there isn't already a light fixture at this point, stretch two strings diagonally across the ceiling from corner to corner; where they intersect is the center point.

2 *Adapt the ceiling rose*
If the rose is to be used with an existing pendant light, you may have to drill a hole through the middle of it to take the wire (some roses come with a hole ready drilled). Turn off the electricity at the main switch, and remove the bulb, fixture and shade or, if necessary, the cover.

Relief detail △
Here, the decorative moldings are picked out in apricot, while the ceiling is painted a paler shade of the same color. See below for how to fix a rose with a heavy fixture.

3 *Prepare the ceiling* △
Cut a paper template that is slightly smaller than the rose and use it to mark off the area to be prepared. If the ceiling is painted, lightly rub down with sandpaper so that the adhesive will get a good grip. Any wallcovering should be stripped. If you've just papered, cut around the marked area with a sharp knife and peel the paper away. If the paper is old, try to strip it dry – only soak if necessary as you may damage surrounding paper.
If installing a plaster rose, knock or probe the ceiling with a bradawl to find the joists and mark the positions.

4 *Install the ceiling rose* △
Spread a layer of adhesive all around the outer rim on the back of the rose with a filling knife. Feed the wire through the hole in the rose (replacing the cover if it has been removed). Then press the rose firmly into position; wipe off any adhesive that squeezes out with a damp sponge.
For extra support, drive panel pins in at an angle through the face of a plastic-type rose – three or four pins should be sufficient. Install a plaster rose to the ceiling joists with rust-proof nails or screws, then fill in the holes with ordinary all-purpose filler.

5 *Paint the rose*
Paint the rose the same color as walls or ceiling, or accentuate the decoration by picking out the relief details in a contrasting color. A matte or silky finish looks better than gloss, while a water-based paint is less likely to clog up the moldings than an oil-based paint. Apply two coats of paint with a small artist's brush.
Replace fixture, bulb and shade.

INSTALLING FIXTURES

When installing a light fixture:
☐ unscrew and remove the base plate, and disconnect the wire
☐ mark the rose and drill holes for the wire and screws that support the light fixture.
☐ apply adhesive, thread wire through center hole and reconnect wires. Press into position.
☐ replace the light, screwing the fixture's baseplate through the rose into the joist.

HANGING RELIEF WALLCOVERINGS

Relief decorations give walls and ceilings an attractive, textured finish, and help to disguise poor surfaces.

If you want to decorate your walls and ceilings with plain color rather than pattern, but you fancy a surface with texture instead of the smoothness of painted plaster, then relief decorations may be the answer. They provide a surface embossed with a pattern that may be regular or random, and are designed to be painted over once they have been hung, giving a relatively permanent finish. There are several qualities and weights to choose from.

LOW-RELIEF PAPER
The least expensive type is known as low-relief or dry-embossed paper, or by Crown's trade name, Anaglypta Original (now often used as a generic term). It consists of two layers of paper bonded together with adhesive and embossed by passing it between steel rollers while the adhesive is still wet. Anaglypta is hung with an all-purpose adhesive, and care must be taken not to fill the hollows on the back of the paper or overstretching will occur. It's important to let the paste soak into the paper after it has been pasted so it becomes supple and easier to hang; the manufacturers will recommend a time, but 10 minutes is about average.

HIGH-RELIEF PAPER
Deep-embossed papers, such as Anaglypta Supadurable, are more expensive than Anaglypta Original, but are stronger and heavier. They're not actually paper at all, since they're made from cotton fibers rather than wood pulp, and can take a far deeper emboss than Anaglypta Original.

The design is molded into the paper while it is still wet, which ensures that the embossing is retained after pasting and hanging. This means that these papers are much easier for the amateur to handle. (With some of the more heavily embossed Anaglypta Original-type wallcoverings the relief tends to flatten unless great care is taken during the hanging process.) Again, an all-purpose adhesive containing a fungicide should be used, and each length should be soaked for the time the manufacturer recommends.

BLOWN VINYLS
Blown vinyl wallcoverings are made from a molded layer of vinyl bonded to a paper backing; Anaglypta Luxury Vinyl and Anaglypta Fine Vinyl are good examples of this type of wallcovering. The vinyl layer is heated during production to make it expand slightly, giving the raised parts a spongy texture.

Because it is blown rather than embossed, and has a paper backing, there are no hollows on the back; this makes pasting easier, and there is no need to soak the length before hanging it. Ready-pasted types are available, otherwise use an all-purpose paste containing a fungicide. Stripping blown vinyls is much easier than stripping other relief papers, because the vinyl surface layer is peeled from the paper backing like an ordinary vinyl wallcovering.

LINCRUSTA
Lincrusta is a heavy, solid embossed wallcovering made from oxidized linseed oil and fillers bonded to a paper backing; it was first manufactured in the late 19th century. It is intended primarily for use on the dado (below the chair rail) particularly in hallways, as it gives such a durable finish.

The linoleum-like surface is embossed while it is still soft, and is then allowed to dry out and harden for about 14 days. The result is an immensely durable wallcovering with a high relief that can be redecorated almost indefinitely. This is just as well, since getting it off again can be extremely difficult. It is hung with a special adhesive called Lincrusta glue. Most types have a selvage that has to be trimmed off before hanging.

DIMENSIONS AND FINISHES
All these relief wallcoverings come in standard-size rolls that measure 33ft. long and about 20½in. wide, although some Lincrustas are made in narrower widths as well for ease of handling. Lincrusta is also available in panels of various sizes.

Most relief wallcoverings can be painted with either water-based or oil-based paints (semi-gloss finish or high gloss). Lincrusta should only be painted with an oil-based paint, and looks most effective decorated with an oil-based glaze tinted with color.

▷ *Glowing colors*
A rich red painted finish is a traditional choice for this Edwardian style Lincrusta dado. Gloss paint emphasizes the heavy molding as light catches on the raised areas.

SURFACE PREPARATION

If you are planning to hang relief decorations over bare wallboard or painted walls, they should be thoroughly washed down and sized. However, old wallcoverings and lining paper should always be stripped off (see Preparing Walls). With Lincrusta, care must be taken to remove any flaky paint before hanging lining paper, since the adhesive is likely to pull this away.

It's a good idea to hang lining paper before putting up any type of relief decoration, as this provides a uniformly absorbent surface on new or repaired wallboard, and helps the paste to dry out on non-absorbent painted surfaces. Hang the lining paper horizontally on walls and, on ceilings, at right angles to the final paper direction. Use paste containing a fungicide if you're hanging blown vinyl paper or Lincrusta. For more details, see Hanging Wallcoverings, pages 61-64.

HANGING LINCRUSTA

1 *Prepare the walls △*
Start by preparing the walls: old wallcoverings should be removed, paint washed down and cracks repaired. All flaky paint should be removed. Since Lincrusta is difficult to trim to fit into awkward corners, it is a good idea to fit new baseboards and chair (or picture) rails to give neat, smooth edges to butt the Lincrusta against. Walls should be cross lined (papered horizontally with lining paper) to give an evenly porous surface.

2 *Cut the drops △*
Handle Lincrusta with care to avoid damaging or cracking its surface. Start by cutting lengths to fit the area to be covered: they should be 2in. longer than the longest drop. Ensure that the pattern matches on each drop. Trim the selvage, using a sharp craft knife and a steel straight-edge: it's easiest to do this on the floor, with a sheet of hardboard underneath the edges being trimmed. Undercut the selvages slightly by angling the blade inwards to ensure perfect joins.

3 *Soak the backing △*
Sponge the paper backing of each length with warm water, and leave it flat to soak for 20 to 30 minutes. Place the lengths back to back in pairs for the best results. This helps the material to expand fully before hanging, and so prevents blisters from forming when the lengths are hung. After the soaking period, wipe off any surplus water with a dry cloth.

4 *Get it straight △*
Use the plumb bob and line to plumb a line on the wall surface at your starting point, and hold the first length up before pasting so you can mark the cutting line at each side. Then trim through the two marks to get a perfect fit at the chair rail, picture rail or ceiling level; leave the bottom edge of the length for trimming after hanging.

5 *Cut around obstructions △*
If there are other obstructions such as light switches and window openings, get a helper to hold the length in place while you mark their positions. If the obstruction is close to the edge of the wallcovering this can be done freehand. Otherwise, measure the position of the obstruction and mark on the Lincrusta. Cut out as marked.

6 *Paste the Lincrusta △*
Brush the Lincrusta glue onto the back of the first length using an old 3in. wide paintbrush.

If the glue is too thick to spread easily, stir it vigorously. Make sure that the whole surface is evenly covered and pay particular attention to the edges.

7 Hang the first drop
Hang the length immediately after pasting is complete, aligning the trimmed top edge with the chair rail, picture rail or ceiling line and one side edge with your plumbed line. Press it into position with a warm wet cloth, working from top to bottom.

Keep the edge level with the plumbed line, and be careful not to bend the Lincrusta at the lower edge. Continue until the Lincrusta is stuck in position to about 8in. above the baseboard.

8 Trim the bottom edge ▷
At the bottom of the length, mark the level of the baseboard at each side. Then place a strip of hardboard against the wall behind the bottom edge and cut through the two marks using your knife and straightedge. Press the bottom edge back into place on the wall.

Wipe off surplus adhesive from paint job or the surface of the Lincrusta with a sponge as you hang each length. Hang subsequent lengths in the same way, butt-joining the lengths as accurately as possible.

9 Dealing with corners
Because of its thickness, Lincrusta is very difficult to hang around corners unless they are fairly well rounded. It may be possible with some thinner types, depending on the design, but it is generally better with sharp corners to cut the length that turns the corner and to butt-join the two sections to obtain a neater finish.

10 Finishing the job
Leave the Lincrusta to dry out for at least 24 hours, and preferably for a couple of days. Then wipe the surface down with a clean cloth dipped in mineral spirits to remove any greasy finger marks or dirt that could spoil the paint finish.

DECORATING RELIEF WALLCOVERINGS

You can decorate relief wallcoverings with any good quality paint, but Lincrusta should be painted with an oil-based (matte or gloss) paint. For a sheen finish, which emphasizes the texture of the wallcovering, use semi-gloss, or choose gloss for a tougher finish.

However, for a more interesting finish, you could apply a scumbled finish: scumbling is a technique that leaves color mainly in the recesses of the surface and so helps to enhance its three-dimensional look.

Scumble is a transparent oil glaze to which mineral spirits and various tints are added to produce a semi-transparent finish. Alternatively, the glaze can be colored with artists' oil colors or any ordinary oil-based paint, such as flat or gloss.

Make up enough to complete the job, since color-matching extra batches could be difficult. Prime the surface with a coat of oil-based flat paint and allow to dry before scumbling. Choose a color several shades lighter than the glaze. The glaze should be thinned before use with a little mineral spirits to make it easier to apply.

Before starting work on the wall itself, it's a good idea to practice the technique on some scraps so you can get a feel for how much glaze to apply and how much pressure to use to wipe it off again and achieve the desired effect. Work with a friend, one of you applying the scumble, the other wiping it off, to speed things up, so the glaze doesn't dry in patches.

BRIGHT IDEA

Childproof walls In children's rooms, it is the lower part of the walls that gets most wear and tear (with drawings, sticky fingers and so on). To protect the walls as much as possible, put up a chair rail and hang a heavily embossed or blown vinyl paper on the dado. Then paint with gloss paint.

This means that you can repaint the lower part of the wall when necessary without having to go to the trouble of redecorating the whole room.

APPLYING SCUMBLE

1 *Brushing on the glaze*
Start by brushing the glaze onto an area of about 1sq.yd. Brush it well into the design to ensure an even coating, but not too thickly or it will run.

2 *Wiping off* ▷
Use a clean, dry, lint-free and colorfast cotton cloth, folded into a pad, to wipe the scumble off the high spots. Wipe lightly then increase the pressure to get the effect you want. Finish by wiping downwards.

3 *Move to the next section*
Repeat the process for subsequent sections, trying to keep a wet edge going so the joins do not show. Remember that the final wipe should be downwards on each section to ensure a matching finish.

4 *Protect the surface*
Leave the scumbled surface to dry for about 24 hours. Then apply a coat of clear varnish – satin gives a softer finish than gloss – to protect the surface and make it completely washable.

◁ *Out of the shadows*
The scumbling technique shows up clearly here: you can see how the greatest depth of color collects in the recesses of the blown vinyl wallcovering. The gray-blue shade chosen gives the wall an almost metallic sheen.

▷ *Hall stories*
Two different patterns of Anaglypta Original have been used to great effect in this hallway. Below the chair rail, the pattern has been painted in a silk finish paint to match the woodwork. Above the rail, a border pattern has been painted to match the wall above. The border pattern is particularly effective when used on the ceiling to imitate a cornice.

WALLCOVERINGS

Wallcoverings used to be available just in paper, now you can choose from many different materials, types and textures.

Once you have decided to cover the walls of your home with a wallcovering, there are certain decisions to make before going shopping.

The type that you choose must be right for the room in which it is to go: kitchens and bathrooms need something to stand up to steam and condensation; landings and hallways, or rooms with several doors leading off them, receive most wear and tear, so cover these walls with a fairly hard-wearing wallcovering. Dining area and kitchen walls are most likely to become stained with food, so a washable or spongeable wallcovering is ideal.

The state of the walls If the wallboard is old and bumpy a thick relief or textured covering conceals the faults. Thin papers are best on newer, smoother surfaces. An all-over pattern also helps to hide defects by distracting the eye.

The cost Prices vary from the cheapest wallpaper to the most expensive natural fabric wallcovering. Decide whether you want something that is going to last, in which case an expensive wallcovering is money well spent; or whether you may want a change in a year or two, in which case look at cheaper papers.

CHECKLIST
☐ Most double roll bolts of wallcovering contain 50-60sq.ft.
☐ If using a patterned wallcovering, check how far apart the pattern repeat is; the larger the pattern, the more waste has to be allowed for.
☐ The wallcovering's wrapper should tell you if it can be washed, scrubbed or sponged, or if it is ready-pasted.
☐ Although wallpapers are hung with standard wallpaper paste, many other sorts of wallcoverings require a special adhesive. Ask your retailer for advice.

WALLCOVERING GROUPS

WHITES
These are designed to be painted over after hanging. They then become semi-permanent, as future decorating need only consist of a fresh coat of paint each time.

Relief paper This type of paper has a pattern embossed in it to give a raised effect on the surface. Anaglypta is a typical example, it comes in relief patterns ranging from weaves to florals. Supadurable is a much thicker paper made with cotton fibers to give it more pronounced relief.

It's important to let the paste soak into relief paper so it becomes supple and easier to hang but care must be taken not to fill the hollows on the back or stretching will occur.

Lincrusta is a rather different type of relief wallcovering. It is very thick and heavyweight, made from linseed oil and fillers mounted on a backing paper. It is deeply embossed, usually with a pattern echoing the period when it was invented – the Edwardian era. It is expensive but durable and must be hung with special adhesive.

Lincrusta

Deep relief   Wood chip   Relief

Woodchip paper Also known as ingrain paper, it consists of wood particles sandwiched between two thin sheets of paper, giving a lumpy, porridge-like surface. It is ideal for covering bad plaster. Better grades are white, and can be left for a time without painting; but they soon start to yellow.

Lining paper (not shown), is a thin paper that should be hung to line walls before hanging expensive or heavyweight wallcoverings, or if the walls are rough and uneven. For lining purposes it should be hung horizontally.

PRINTED PAPERS
This is by far the largest group of wallcovering. It includes all the papers available that are printed in thousands of patterns and colorways. Depending on what you choose, the price range is as wide as the choice of designs.

Machine-printed wallcoverings. The pattern and design on this type is printed by machine. The price reflects the thickness of the paper and the number of different colors used, The pattern or design can either be simply printed on the surface of the paper or stamped into it to give an embossed or textured effect.

Hand-printed wallpapers offer superb designs and colors, but they are usually much more expensive than machine-printed papers. The colors can sometimes smear if wetted by paste and because hand-printing is not as accurate as machine printing, getting a pattern to match between two lengths can be tricky.

Sometimes the plain paper edging down each side of the roll is left untrimmed by the manufacturer, although most reputable specialist shops trim them for you before selling them.

Machine-printed   Hand-printed

PVC coated (not shown) Many printed papers are coated with a thin layer of plastic to make them washable or spongeable. The thicker the coating, the more it repels water, so the thinnest coatings are only spongeable. However, even those with the thickest plastic coating should not be scrubbed as this can damage the coating.

Remember that as they repel water they can be very hard to strip, so make sure when buying that you choose one that is dry-strippable (which means the paper can be stripped off the wall without soaking with water first).

VINYL WALLCOVERINGS

The design on this group of wallcoverings is not printed directly onto a roll of paper, but onto a thin layer of vinyl, which is then fused to a paper backing.

Although usually more expensive than wallpaper, vinyls are very popular, because they are not only washable but often scrubbable too.

Many vinyls are ready-pasted: the back is coated with dry paste that is activated when lengths are dipped in a trough of water. This makes hanging easy and does away with messy paste, pasting table and brush.

If the type you buy is not ready-pasted, be sure to paste it with fungicidal adhesive. Vinyl is non-porous, so it doesn't allow the wall behind it to breathe. This means any moisture in the wall is trapped and the wall or paper may become moldy.

Vinyl can be stripped dry, so if you want to take it down you simply peel away the decorative vinyl layer, leaving the paper backing behind. This makes a good foundation for a wallcovering.

Blown vinyl   Standard vinyl

Standard vinyls are perfect if you want a printed wallcovering that is going to last longer and stand up to more wear and tear than ordinary wallpaper. There are thousands of designs and colors available as well as different effects.
Blown vinyls A blown vinyl is produced by a heat process that makes the vinyl expand to give a blown, raised effect. The first blown vinyls were produced in off-white shades designed for overpainting, so they could also be grouped under 'whites.' But colored and patterned ones are now proving very popular. Although a blown vinyl has a raised effect the backing layer remains flat, so it is much easier to paste and hang.

FABRICS AND NATURAL MATERIALS

Many printed and embossed wallcoverings imitate fabrics, textiles and natural materials, but it is possible to hang the real thing, although it tends to be more expensive.

An unbacked fabric wallcovering is wider than a standard wallcovering width and designed to be hung on walls by stretching it around partitions or backing panels first and then mounting these onto your walls. (You are really only likely to need unbacked fabric if you have very uneven walls, such as those found in old houses and cottages.)

By far the easiest way of hanging fabric on your walls is to buy a fabric wallcovering that is backed with either paper, plastic or latex. These are much more expensive than ordinary wallpapers. They usually come in standard widths and should be hung with special adhesives. (Ask your retailer for advice on which adhesive is suitable.)
Cork A cork wallcovering is made from thin sheets of real bark from the cork oak tree, glued onto a paper backing. The cork is available in its natural colors or dyed. The swirling grain of the bark gives each piece a unique natural pattern.

Cork, however, is prone to crumbling so it is

Paper-backed cork   Textile   Hessian

not terribly easy to hang nor is it that suitable to hang on walls that are likely to receive a lot of wear and tear.
Hessian is one of the most popular fabric wallcoverings if you want to create a rustic look. It is available in a range of colors and comes paper- or latex-backed.
Other textiles There are many other paper or vinyl-backed woven textile wallcoverings ranging from real silk and wool to synthetic fibers. Look for those that are coated in vinyl and therefore washable.

SPECIAL EFFECTS

This group covers other types of wallcoverings not already mentioned, because they are unique in the way they look and the methods by which they are made.
Foil wallcoverings consist of a thin layer of metallized plastic film on a paper backing. They reflect every speck of light to create a shiny mirror effect. They can be machine- or hand-printed and must be hung with a special adhesive. They are expensive, but ideal for small areas that receive little natural light. They should be hung only on flat walls, as the slightest dent or bump shows up. Metal foil conducts electricity and so should not be tucked behind light switches.
Foam polyethylene This decorative wallcovering is unlike any other. The design is printed onto foamed plastic, which is lightweight and therefore easy to hang.

The paste is applied to the wall, not the wallcovering, either with a paint roller or large brush, and the wallcovering is hung straight from the roll – there is no need to cut it to length first.

It is warm to the touch and, unlike vinyl, allows the wall behind to breathe. This makes it a good choice for kitchens or bathrooms where condensation is a problem. Its light weight makes it easy to hang in stairwells and on ceilings. Like

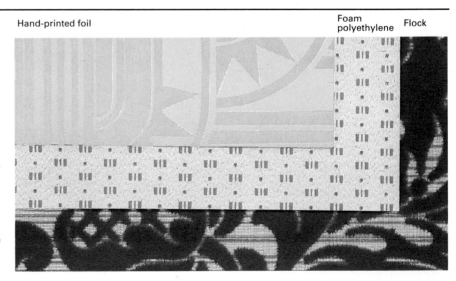

Hand-printed foil   Foam polyethylene   Flock

vinyls it is washable and dry-strippable, but not as tough.
Flock This has the luxurious look and feel of velvet. The rich pile is produced not by weaving but by gluing short lengths of silk or other fibers to a paper backing, then cutting a design into it.
The designs are usually traditional Victorian and Edwardian formalized florals or stripes, in rich red, green and gold colors. Traditional flocks are hard to hang as paste smears ruin the pile; but vinyl versions are easier and may even come ready-pasted. Both should be brushed regularly.

CORNICES AND COVE MOLDING

A cornice adds the finishing touch to any room, and hides unsightly gaps between the walls and ceiling.

A cornice is any continuous length of horizontal molding between walls and ceiling. Cove molding is the name given to the prefabricated molding used to make a cornice. Traditional cornices are often elaborate and richly embossed. Modern cornices are usually a simple length of concave cove molding.

As well as providing a decorative break between the walls and ceiling, and hiding gaps, a cornice can also be used to conceal plumbing and wiring.

HOW CORNICES ARE MADE

Cornices can be made from plaster, wood or cove molding which is constructed from expanded plastic foam, plasterboard or polystyrene.

Plaster Elaborate cornices found in period homes are usually made from molded plaster. It is possible to buy new lengths of plaster cove molding but the material is difficult and heavy to work with and expensive.

Wood Some traditional carved cornices are made from wood, either painted or stained. It is difficult to replace this type of cornice without using the services of an expert woodcarver.

Expanded plastic foam If a traditional plaster cornice is very badly damaged, it may be possible to replace it with a re-production design made in rigid expanded plastic foam. The material has a lightweight core, a hard, smooth surface, and comes in many styles. It is light in weight, easy to fit and can be cut, drilled and sanded. The more elaborate the design, the more this type of cornice costs but even the most expensive designs are cheaper than the same thing

Period elegance
A carefully restored cornice adds a touch of authentic elegance to this cool blue living room. A similar effect can be achieved with modern reproduction cove molding.

in plaster. This type of cornice can be left unpainted, or colored to match the room scheme.

Plasterboard Plasterboard cove molding can be used to make a simple cornice. It has a plaster core sheathed in a thick paper skin. It comes only as a plain concave quadrant with a hollow back, is fairly heavy and has no surface detail. It needs to be painted.

Polystyrene Available in similar style to plasterboard cove molding, polystyrene is light in weight and has a slightly textured surface. It is easy to fit, comes with separate pre-formed internal and external miter pieces and is inexpensive. It must be painted.

MEASURING UP

Cove molding for use in adding or re-placing a cornice is sold in lengths – usually of 2 or 3yds. Heavy plaster cornice is sold in short lengths or is made specially to measure.

Begin by finding out the lengths the cove molding you have chosen comes in

then measure the perimeter of the room and work out how many pieces will be needed. Remember that you have to cut corner cove molding joints in most types, which will entail some waste.

SURFACE PREPARATION

Unless you are using a wood or light-weight polystyrene cove molding, you will need to strip wallcovering from the area of wall and ceiling where the cove molding will fit. If this is not done the molding could fall down. If the wall is painted, wash it down and rub the area where the molding is to be fitted with sandpaper to provide a base for the adhesive.

TOOLS AND EQUIPMENT

Cutting Use a saw for plaster, plasterboard, expanded plastic foam and wood and a craft knife for polystyrene.

Measuring Equip yourself with a metal rule. If you are using plasterboard, plaster, wood or expanded plastic foam, you will need a miter box. For small moldings, use an ordinary carpenter's

miter box. For larger types, make a box, (see Step 5).

Installing For lightweight cove molding use the adhesive recommended by the maker. If the design is a heavy plaster molded type, you will need masonry pins, wall plugs and screws, or frame plugs. This is a job for two, working from two pairs of step ladders with a plank across.

CHECK YOUR NEEDS

- ☐ Tape measure
- ☐ Metal ruler and pencil
- ☐ Craft knife or saw
- ☐ Wallpaper scraper
- ☐ Miter box
- ☐ Adhesive and adhesive spreader
- ☐ Filling knife
- ☐ Masonry pins, screws and wallplugs or frame plugs, plus drill, screwdriver or hammer for heavy types.
- ☐ Latex paint and brush

---

1 *Make a guideline* ▽
Using a length of cove molding held into the wall/ceiling angle as a guide, mark a guideline all around the room. Use a soft pencil to make the mark. This will help you to align the molding as you hang it and also indicates the area of old wallcovering to be stripped if the walls or ceilings are papered.

2 *Mark the surface* ▽
If wallcovering has to be stripped, go over these lines with a metal rule and craft knife, butting through into the wallboard beneath. This will make a distinct line but don't worry as it will be covered once the cornice is in place. Keep the line as straight as possible and don't dig in too hard with the knife.

3 *Strip the paper* ▽
Dry-strip as much of the covering as you can from the wall and ceiling surfaces between the lines, by lifting seams between lengths. Don't soak it unless you have to, since you risk damaging the wallcovering further down the wall. It doesn't matter if some paper or old adhesive remains on the surface.

---

4 *Painted surfaces*
If the wall is painted, wash it down using a solution of soap in water (follow manufacturer's instructions) to remove surface grease and dirt. Don't use too much water on the wall or it will run down and mark the paint job below the ruled area. Leave the wall to dry then sand down between the marked lines with medium grade sandpaper, or with an electric sander. This will roughen the surface providing a base for the adhesive. Wash down to remove loose dust and let the wall dry. If you try to adhere molding to a damp or dusty wall the adhesive will not cling.

5 *Make a miter box* ▷
If you are using large or ornate molding, time can be saved and mistakes avoided by making a miter box to match the coving size. Make it about 18in. long, from wood about ¾in. thick, which is glued and screwed together, and wide enough so the molding sits in the box just as it will in the floor/ceiling angle, with the edge of the cove molding that will rest upon the ceiling resting squarely on the base and the wall face against the box sides nearest you. Use a protractor to mark two saw guides at a 45-degree angle facing in opposite directions. Cut them right down to the base of the box.

6 Measuring and cutting
Start at a corner. Unless miters are ready cut you'll need to cut your own. The way the miter is cut – from right to left, or left to right – depends on whether the corner is external or internal and which side of the miter you are cutting (see Step 11). To cut the miter correctly make two templates using scraps of cove molding. Mark which face is to go against ceiling. Miter one piece of the miter box at one end, cutting from left to right. Make a parallel cut at other end. Miter both ends of second piece but this time from right to left. When mitering the molding, put the templates in the appropriate corner to see which way to cut. When cutting miters for external corners, the molding must be a bit longer than the wall.

7 Fitting the first piece ▽
Spread adhesive onto the back face of the first length. Hold in position on the wall and ceiling, checking that the edges are aligned with your guide line, and press firmly into position. Hold in place for a couple of minutes to give the adhesive a chance to grip.

8 Extra support
For heavy molding, use masonry pins at 24in. intervals. Position the molding, drill holes and insert frame plugs (long wallplugs that are pushed into the molding and screwed into the wall).

9 Make a neat finish ▷
When the length is firmly in position, use your filling knife to remove any excess adhesive that has squeezed out along the edges of the length of molding. This should automatically fill any gaps between the wall or ceiling and the edge of the molding caused by uneven surfaces. When using the putty knife, be careful not to mark the edge of the cornice or the wall or ceiling. If there are any gaps too wide to be covered by the adhesive, fill them with a fine-grade speckle and smooth neatly. The filler can be sanded down for a fault-free finish.

10 Fitting the next length
Now miter and fit a second length at the other end of the same wall. If the two lengths are longer than the wall, hold the second length in place after cutting the miter on one end and mark the point at which it overlaps the second length. Make a straight square ended cut at this point, then apply adhesive and press the length into place. Use adhesive to fill the joint between the two lengths. Wipe off any smears. If the wall is longer than two lengths of molding, simply fill in the gap between the first and second lengths with one or more square-ended lengths as necessary.

11 Dealing with corners
Where two internal corner pieces meet, you may find it easier to push adhesive into the join with your finger or using a small piece of wood. It is important to get enough adhesive on the corner pieces to make a gap-free joint. All corner joints should be finished off neatly with a putty knife to make a good sharp join. This is important on external corners as gaps are most noticeable here. Wipe surplus adhesive away from the corners before it sets using a damp brush or a sponge.

12 Moving around the room
The diagram below left shows how molding is cut to fit a typical room. If possible, avoid having a short piece in the center of a chimney breast. If short pieces are needed on other walls, they should be centered between long lengths.

CLEANING AND RESTORATION
In older homes it is common to find a beautifully molded cornice so thick with paint that the detail has almost disappeared. It is possible to restore the cornice – providing that you have the time and the patience to embark on a painstaking paint stripping operation.
Identify the problem Start by trying to identify the paint used. If the surface is glossy, it's probably oil-based gloss paint. If the surface is matte and chalky, it may be either water-based latex or oil-based paint. If the surface is matte but sound, a modern latex paint has probably been used for the top coat.
Oil-base paint Either can be removed using paste or a gel stripper. If you are

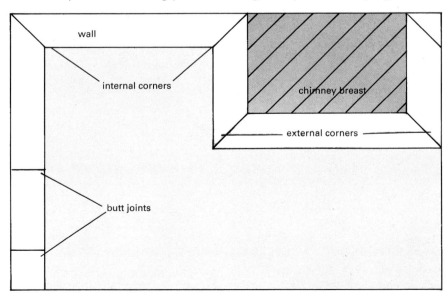

wall

internal corners

chimney breast

external corners

butt joints

using gel stripper, wear gloves and goggles as it burns skin if spilled. You can use a hot-air stripper but it is rather tiring to hold the gun and work a scraper on the cornice as you are constantly reaching upwards.

Flaking Try water first. If the surface is water-based it will scrape away. Use a plant sprayer to keep the surface wet as you work (see right).

Latex paint This requires a chemical stripper. Some paint strippers won't work on latex so be sure to choose one that will (the instructions on the back of the can or packet will tell you).

Work slowly This is back-breaking work, so plan to do the job over several days. Remember that you may come across any combination of these paint types, so you will have to be prepared to switch your methods.

REPAIRING DAMAGE

You may find localized damage to the plaster molding as you remove the paint. Patch or restore this using a quick-setting material such as alabastine or plaster of Paris.

If large sections of detail are missing, make a mold using an undamaged area as your model.

Spread the inside of the mold with silicone grease and use quick-setting filler to form the new piece. When set, stick in place with epoxy-resin adhesive.

You may wish to replace plaster cornices with new wood moldings or other light-weight material.

PAINTING THE CORNICE

Once the cornice is in place or stripped, it can be painted. Use latex, thinning the first coat on plaster and wallboard with about 10 percent extra water. Add a second coat when the first coat is dry. To avoid filling in the detail on ornate types, apply two thin coats rather than one thick one.

You may decide to redecorate ornate molding using colored paint to pick out detail. Apply overall background color as described. Apply color using a small artist's brush, supported on a mahlstick – an 18in. length of doweling with a small ball of foam wrapped in cloth at the end (see right). This helps to steady your hand. The small test cans of latex sold by the major paint manufacturers are ideal.

An eye for detail
Using simple modern cove molding to create a cornice adds the essential finishing touch to this room. The cornice and baseboard are painted cream to contrast with the blue color scheme and to match the furniture.

BRIGHT IDEA

Hidden fixtures Most modern moldings are hollow at the back allowing you to conceal wiring. Make sure the molding you buy will fit over whatever you are trying to conceal. A variation on this idea is to use molding to hide slimline fluorescent tubes that beam up to the ceiling. The molding is positioned about 3in. down from the ceiling and only attached to the walls. This leaves a space for the light to shine upwards and for tubes to be replaced. Specially made molding is available from lighting specialists.

ATTACHING FABRIC TO WALLS

Fabric-lined walls give a luxurious air to living rooms and bedrooms and can disguise damaged walls.

If you want to create warmth and softness in a room; fabric-lined walls may well be the answer. In a similar way to tongue-and-groove cladding, fabric can be used to cover up poor plaster-work, and for real warmth you can add insulation under the fabric. However, it can be a fairly expensive business as fabric costs more per square foot than most wallcoverings, and for the technique described here, with fabric gathered onto curtain rods, the gathering means you will need even more fabric.

Shirring fabric onto rods means that you can actually take the fabric down for cleaning from time to time. It does involve a fair amount of sewing, particularly if you want to add a border in a contrasting color.

CHOOSE YOUR FABRICS

Plain fabrics or small patterns give the best effects when covering walls. Large patterns can be overpowering, and you have to be very careful to match up the motifs when joining widths. Pleat the fabric in your hands before buying to test the effect. Go for fabrics that are as wide and cheap as possible; but avoid ones that fade (e.g., dressmaking fabrics) if the room gets direct sunlight.

Calculating fabric quantities To calculate fabric quantities you will need to draw a sketch of each wall to be covered. Divide the walls into rectangular areas, with each rectangle as large as possible.

For example, on a wall with a pair of windows, you will have floor to ceiling rectangles on either side and between the windows, with smaller rectangles above and below the windows. For each rectangle you will need a panel of fabric at least one-and-a-half times the width, and measuring the height of the rectangle plus 3in. for casings top and bottom.

TOOLS AND EQUIPMENT

For fabric shirred onto curtain rods you will need enough rods to run all the way across the upper and lower edge of each rectangle. If the plasterwork is bad or if your walls are difficult to nail, you will find it easier to install furring strips before fixing the curtain rod brackets. Use ½in. diameter metal curtain rod; or, as a cheaper alternative, curtain wires held with screw eyes fixed to furring strips.

Note Radiators create problems: if you can remove them, fit the fabric behind, then replace the radiators, slitting the fabric where the brackets are positioned. If not, box them in beforehand. Take this into account when measuring up and deciding where to install furring strips and curtain rods.

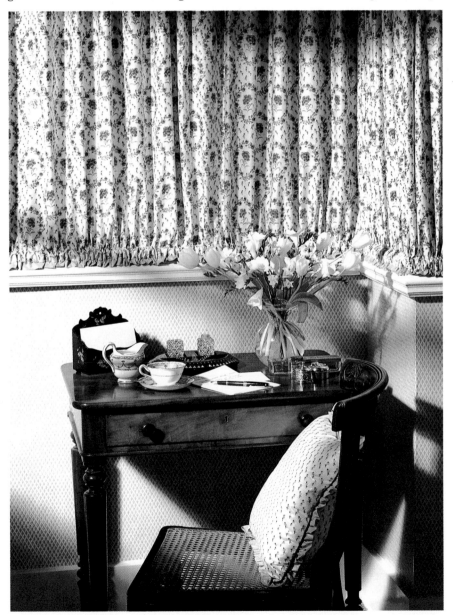

CHECK YOUR NEEDS
☐ 2 × 1in. furring strips (optional)
☐ Screws and wallplugs
☐ Drill and screwdriver
☐ Fabric
☐ Sewing machine, needle, thread
☐ Curtain rods and brackets

Patterned and pleated
An effective way to use patterned fabric on a wall: the design is a delicate one, and the fabric stops short at the chair rail. A lime green border emphasizes the effect and picks up the green in fabric and wallcovering.

79

MEASURING YOUR ROOM

Before you start you need to measure the room so that you can work out the amount of furring strips, the length of curtain rods and the yardage of fabric.

1 *Draw plans of the walls* ▷
Measure each wall and draw a sketch showing all the major obstacles (windows, doors, and so on). Mark the overall measurements, with the dimensions of the obstacles. Then divide each wall into a series of rectangles, as shown by the dotted lines in the diagrams on the right.

2 *Calculate amount of furring*
If you plan to attach furring strips before hanging the curtain rods, measure the upper and lower edge of each rectangle to give the total length of furring required.

3 *Amount of curtain rod*
You need the same amount of curtain rod as furring. At this stage plan where the brackets are to go: position them to coincide with the corners of the rectangles. It's neater if you use the minimum number of sections of rod (see Step 1 opposite).

4 *Calculate the fabric*
For each rectangle on your plan you will need a panel of fabric 1½ times the width of the rectangle, and the same depth as the rectangle plus a total of 6½in. for making up the casings.

ATTACHING THE FURRING

It is easier to hang the curtain rods accurately if you put up furring strips around the room first. Curtain rods have quite small screws, so it is easier to screw them straight onto wood, rather than into the wallboard with wall plugs.

1 *Cut lengths of furring*
Consult your plan (see above) and cut lengths of furring to fit each section to be covered.

2 *Dealing with external corners* ▷
At external corners, allow for extra furring so you can extend one length to overlap the end of the adjacent length for a neat finish.

3 *Boxing in radiators* ◁
If you are going to box in your radiators you can buy custom-built covers, or build your own. Make an open box from 1 × 5in. planed softwood. You will need a piece for each side, scribed to fit around the baseboard at the bottom, and a piece to go across the top of the radiator. Glue and screw at the corners, strengthening the joints with angle irons

if necessary. For the front, nail fabric or decorative perforated hardboard to the outer edge of the frame, taking it down to about 4in. from floor level to allow convection currents to circulate. Glue and nail beading around the edge of the fabric or hardboard for a neat finish. Fix mirror plates to the back edges of the side panels of the box (two on each side) and screw the whole structure firmly to the wall.

4 *Organizing the outlets* ▷
Since the fabric is to be held on furring strips, it will stand a couple of inches away from the wall. It will be much neater if you arrange for an electrician to come and reposition the switches so they are raised from the wall. It is also advisable to move them slightly, if necessary, so that they are right at the edge of the wall – light switches up against the architrave, and outlets butting up to the baseboard. At the same time, ask the electrician to fit furring strips around the outlets.

5 *Arranging pictures*
Because the fabric stands away from the wall you'll need to put up furring if you want to hang pictures. This means that the fabric will not be distorted when the pictures are hung. If there are just a couple of large pictures to hang, small blocks of wood will be sufficient. If you have sets or groups of pictures to hang, long furring strips will give you a bit of flexibility when it's time to hang them.

6 Prepare the furring ◁
Fit the furring along the upper and lower edges of each area to be covered. They should be as close to the top or bottom of the rectangle as possible. Drill a series of holes, every 20in. or so down the length of the strip. Avoid fitting screws within 1¼in. of each end, to ensure plenty of room for attaching the rods in the corners of the rectangles.

7 Fit the furring
Hold the furring in place, mark the positions of the holes on the walls. Fit a wallplug into each hole. Start a screw in each of the end holes in the furring strip, then screw them into the plugged holes. Add the intervening screws.

ATTACHING FABRIC WITH RODS

When attaching fabric to curtain rods there is a fair amount of straightforward sewing to be done.

1 Hang the rods in position ▷
You will need to hang curtain rods to hold the fabric at the top and bottom of each section of wall to be covered. Where there are more than two lengths of curtain rod, fit brackets back to back so that they are as nearly as possible continuous. Fit the brackets so that the middle of the bracket is about 1¼in. from the upper and lower edges of the wall.

2 Make up panels with casings ▷
Cut sufficient lengths of fabric to make up the width you need. Join widths of fabric where necessary with a flat seam, pressed open. Turn under a ½in. double hem down each long edge. For the casings, turn under 1¼in., then a further 2in., and press. Make two lines of straight machine stitching, one ¾in. from hem line, another 1in. inside that. At this stage, cut and finish the fabric without any allowance for small irregularities such as light switches.

BRIGHT IDEA

WARM IT UP

For extra warmth, you can insulate behind the fabric. This can be done with sheets of polystyrene, or with polyester cloth.

If you are using polystyrene, there's a choice between rolls, which are fairly thin, and stuck up like wallpaper (they are intended for hanging beneath wallcovering) or thicker sheets, which are available in 4×8 foot panels. Make sure that the panels are no thicker than the furring strips. Attach the panels to the wall with one of the special adhesives made for attaching polystyrene.

If you use polyester cloth (available in 32in. widths from dressmaking departments), choose the heaviest weight and simply staple it to the wall so that the whole area inside the furring strip is completely covered.

3 Fit the fabric
Thread the panels onto the curtain rods along the top of each section. Fit the rods so that the fabric panels hang down. Where there are no obstructions (such as light switches) slip the lower rods into the casings and fit the lower rods into their brackets. Distribute the fullness of the fabric evenly and bunch it up slightly at the sides so that the brackets are covered, arranging the fabric so that you don't get any unsightly gaps.

4 Small irregularities ▷
In order to make the fabric fit neatly around obstructions such as light switches, electrical outlets, fireplace corners and so on, you may have to improvise slightly. Where electrical outlets are close to the baseboard, fit a short length of curtain rod. Cut a piece out of the fabric where it hangs over the outlet leaving 3in. allowance to make a casing. Clip into the fabric so that you can turn up a casing as before. Bind the raw edges of the fabric or turn in narrowly to neaten. At light switches, you can either cut into the fabric and staple it to furring strips around the switch or add short pieces of curtain rod and make casings above and below the switch.

When you have dealt satisfactorily with all the irregularities, finish fitting the fabric around the bottom of the room.

WIRED IN

For greater economy, use expanding curtain wires instead of rods. Do not make the rectangles spanned by each wire too wide or there is a danger of the wires sagging in the center. Make the casing channel slightly narrower than for curtain rods (position the rows of stitching ¾ and 1¼in. from the hemline). Attach screw eyes to the furring strips and, where panels meet, fit two screw hooks to each eye, so that you can pull the fabric panels as close together as possible.

Make sure you have the curtain wires as tightly stretched as possible, to avoid sagging.

◁ *Plain and pleated*
Soft peach-colored fabric, finely gathered, makes the perfect wallcovering for a classically elegant room. Again, the fabric ends at the chair rail. The striped paper below the rail picks up the peach tones of the fabric and echoes the vertical pleat lines above.

BASIC TILING TECHNIQUES
Installing ceramic tile is easy and rewarding.

You can use tile in a variety of situations around the house to provide a durable surface that is immune to moisture, household stains and all but the most determined physical abuse. If you've never tiled before, here's everything you need to know to complete the job successfully.

A simple start Don't be overambitious. For your first project start with a small rectangular area of tile supported on a level surface. For example, the back-splash behind a lavatory or along the end side of a tub enclosure or the strip of wall between a kitchen countertop and upper cabinets. You will then get the feel of the technique without worrying about wasting tile or having to master the techniques of cutting out intricate shapes.

What kind of surface? A sound, painted surface can be left alone, but wallpaper, even if painted, must be removed. You can tile over new plaster or drywall, but the surface should be primed with latex primer. Don't attempt to tile over thin tempered hardboard – rigid ceramic tiles may crack if applied to a flexible surface; instead, remove it and replace with particleboard or plywood. If the surface is already firmly tiled, you can apply new tile over the old.

Choosing the right size tile Tile comes in many different sizes, from 1-inch square to 24-inch square.

If you plan to tile between fixed boundaries such as countertops and cabinets, choose a size that will avoid a lot of awkward cutting to size. Most suppliers will sell you a single tile that you can take home and use to check measurements and color matches. Take accurate measurements of the area you want to tile. Then, work out exactly how many tiles you need to cover it. Count cut tiles as whole ones and buy an extra 10% to allow for breakage.

TILING EQUIPMENT

You'll need a few simple tools and materials before you start.

Tile adhesive comes ready-mixed. You'll need a notched adhesive spreader to apply it. Allow 1 lb. per 11 sq. ft.

Tile grout is also sold ready-mixed in cans and caulk tubes. A 2¼lb. container will grout about 7 sq. yd. For a very small area, you can save money by buying a combined adhesive/grout mix.

Tile cutters range from a simple carbide-tipped scoring tool to snap cutters to tile-cutting kits. You can rent tile cutters at tool rental shops.

Nippers are used to nibble away strips of tile less than an inch wide.

A file or whetstone is used to smooth rough edges left by nippers.

Tile spacers – small, plastic crosses you set into the adhesive bed at the corner of each tile – are optional. Whether you need them depends on the spacing requirements of the tile. Many tiles have slightly beveled edges that create a uniform gap between them; others have small lugs on the edges to give the same effect. Only square-edged tiles without lugs need spacers.

A carpenter's level is used to check that the tiles are even.

Plain and fancy
Decorative border tiles teamed with less expensive, matching field tiles add a distinctive touch.

1 *Positioning a panel of tiles* ▽
With a whole panel of tiles, such as a lavatory backsplash (below), find and mark the center of the basin on the wall. Then check where the edges of the tiles will fall either by butting the edges of two tiles to the center line (left) or by marking the center of a tile and positioning it to match the center of the basin (right).

CHECK YOUR NEEDS

☐ Tiles
☐ Adhesive
☐ Notched adhesive spreader
☐ Tile or snap cutter
☐ Nippers (optional)
☐ Tile file or whetstone
☐ Tile spacers (optional)
☐ Metal ruler or try-square
☐ Carpenter's level

☐ Grout
☐ Flexible spreader for grout
☐ Dowel (or unsharpened end of round pencil)
☐ Silicone sealant
☐ Pencil, felt pen
☐ Sponge and dry cloths

Tiling wall to wall ▷
To tile an area wall-to-wall (top right), first lay a row of tiles loose on the surface in front of the area to be tiled and, working from the center as for the lavatory backsplash, position them so you have at least a third of one tile at either end. It is better to cut two tiles at each end than end up with a narrow piece at one end.

Tiling a tub surround ▷
To tile a tub surround, lay out tiles to have whole ones at either end of the run, and any cut tiles in the corners. If necessary, let the end tiles project beyond the tub rather than have narrow cuts at the corners.

2 *Prepare the wall*
Wash down existing tiles or painted surfaces, scraping off any areas of flaking paint. Strip wallcoverings; if you are tiling only part of a papered wall, mark out and strip an area of paper 1in. smaller in each direction than the tiling will occupy. Paint any bare plaster or drywall with primer.

3 *Begin with a level surface*
Use the straight edge of a sink, tub or countertop as a guideline for positioning the tiles horizontally and rest the tiles directly on the surface.

4 *Mark the start* ◁
Use the carpenter's level to draw a true vertical line at the point where tile is going to start.

5 *Apply the adhesive* ◁
Scoop some tile adhesive out of the tub with the notched spreader and press it onto the wall. Draw the spreader firmly across the wall so the teeth ridge the adhesive to a standard thickness. Apply enough adhesive to allow you to position up to six tiles in the first row. Make sure you can see the vertical start line – scrape away a little adhesive if necessary.

6 *Position the first tile*
Rest the bottom edge of the tile on the countertop/basin, holding the tile at a 45-degree angle to the wall (see diagram 7). Align with the vertical starting line and press the tile firmly into the adhesive. Check that it is level using the carpenter's level; if it isn't, twist it slightly until it is, making sure it is still aligned.

7 *Adding more tiles* ▷
Complete the first row in the same way, butting the tile edges closely together or fitting spacers if using square-edged tiles without lugs. If the row runs right up to a corner, leave any cut pieces until later (but scrape off the adhesive where they will go so it doesn't set).

Check that all the tiles are sitting flush with one another; press in any that are sticking out, pry out any that have sunk too deep into the adhesive and put some more adhesive on the wall before re-bedding them.

Add successive rows of whole tiles, checking that the vertical rows are correctly aligned. After placing the final row, clean off any excess adhesive.

8 *Fitting tiles into a corner* △
To fit tiles accurately, turn the tile so that the glazed side faces the wall. Position the tile in the corner, overlapping the adjacent fixed tile; check it is straight. Mark cutting line at top and bottom edges with a pencil, then turn the tile over and draw the line on the glazed side with a felt-tipped pen.

9 *Cutting the tiles* △
Cut the tile by scoring along the line on the glazed side with a tile cutter and metal ruler. Place a matchstick under the tile at each end of the scored line and press firmly downwards on each half of the tile. It will snap cleanly so long as you've scored the glaze thoroughly with your tile cutter.

Test the fit of each cut tile in its gap and then spread adhesive on the back and press it into place. As a general rule, match the uncut edge of a cut tile to the edge of a whole tile. (If you plan to turn the corner and continue tiling you may be able to use the offcut along the new wall so don't throw it away.)

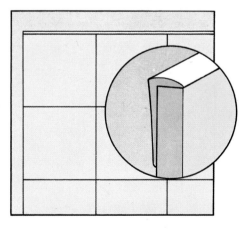

USING A CUTTER KIT
These usually consist of a tile cutter, a try-square, which is used to guide the cutter, and a tool that grips the scored tile in angled jaws and snaps it along the cutting line.

CUTTING A NARROW STRIP
If you have to cut a strip of tile less than an inch wide, score it in the usual way and then use a pair of nippers to nibble off the excess tile. Use a whetstone or file to smooth out any unevenness on the cut edge that may result.

EDGE TRIM
You can finish off top and side edges with a tile trim. Bed the lengths of trim into the adhesive before you fix the last row of tiles and adjust the trim once they have been positioned so it fits snugly over the tile edges.

10 **Remove the spacers**
If you used tile spacers, let the adhesive set for at least two hours before prying them out carefully using a small screwdriver. Take care not to disturb the tiles. Scrape off any adhesive on the surface of the tiles at this stage.

11 **Apply the grout** ▷
Let the tile adhesive set overnight. Then load a small amount of grout onto the flexible spreader (above) and draw it across the joints between tiles, forcing it well in. Use a damp sponge (below) to wipe off any surplus as you complete an area of six tiles.

12 **Finishing off** △
Draw the end of a length of slim doweling along each grout line to leave the surface slightly concave. Leave the grout to dry for as long as the manufacturer recommends, then polish the tile surface clean and bright with a dry cloth.

13 **Seal a backsplash** ◁
Avoid leaking joints by using a flexible silicone sealant to fill narrow gaps (up to ¼in.) between tiles and tops of fixtures. Do not use grouting as it has no elasticity and may crack with movement. First make sure the surfaces are clean and dry. Most sealants are squeezed directly from a tube or with a caulk gun. Use an even pressure and always push the tube away from you along the joint. Trim off excess sealant with a razor blade, smooth by lightly pulling a moist finger along the joint, and leave to set.

BRIGHT IDEA

COLORED GROUTING
Most tile grout is white. If you want to add an extra touch of color, however, you can either use colored grout or brush on special grout paint as soon as the original white grout has dried. Matching the color of the tiles will give a uniform look to the tiled area; a contrast color will emphasize the tiling.

Grout paint can also be used to brighten up old grout that is beginning to look shabby.

Colors you should be able to find include red, green, pink and blue, as well as a range of neutral colors such as gray, ivory and beige.

TILING A COUNTERTOP

Finishing a countertop with tiles can give a completely new look to your kitchen or bathroom.

Ceramic tiles make an attractive and practical countertop for a kitchen or bathroom. They're solid, easy to clean and they should last indefinitely. The edge of the work surface can be finished with a smart matching tile trim, or with a simple wood edging.

In some ways, tiling a countertop is easier than tiling a wall: the area is relatively small, and the surface is horizontal rather than vertical. However, as tiles need to be of the thicker variety and some cutting is almost inevitable, it's advisable to have done a simple wall tiling project before, such as a sink backsplash.

Types of surfaces An existing tiled or plastic laminate surface can be tiled over as long as it's clean, reasonably smooth and firmly fixed. If you're not satisfied with the surface, replace it with a piece of particleboard.

Remove a plastic or metal edging strip: wood edging is best left in place and tiled over.

Choosing the tiles Kitchen countertops need tiles that are strong enough to withstand hard knocks and hot pans –

anything over ¼in. thick is suitable, but bear in mind that the thicker the tiles, the more difficult they are to cut. You can use lighter, thinner tiles on bathroom surfaces. In general, a matte finish is better than a highly glazed one.

Wall tiles offer the greatest choice of design and color. You'll have more limited choices in thicker countertop tiles, but they come with matching trim tiles for finishing the front edge (there are straight lengths and pieces for inside and outside corners).

Mosaic tiles are another option: because they are small, they are easy to fit into a given area although for the same reason they're generally more difficult to cut. It is possible to use ceramic floor tiles but they're thick and very hard to cut; quarry tiles are even thicker and, if unglazed, they must be sealed after laying.

How many tiles? Ceramic tiles range from 1in. to 24in. square. To make sure you buy the size of tile that will fit without too much awkward cutting, it's worth buying a few to experiment with; most suppliers will sell you single tiles.

Alternatively, use cardboard cutouts and add a tiny bit all around to allow for the joints.

Measure the width and length of the area you want to tile. Then, once you know the size of tile you're going to use, you can calculate how many you will need. Buy enough tiles to cover the area with whole tiles, plus a few extra to allow for mistakes.

TOOLS AND EQUIPMENT

Adhesive must be waterproof. If the countertop is uneven – old tiles, for example – use a thick-bed adhesive to cover any irregularities.

Grout must be waterproof. On tiled kitchen countertops, where food is prepared, use an epoxy grout that is non-toxic and resists staining.

A tile cutter, with a wheel to score a cutting line and strong angled jaws to snap the tile, is the best tool for cutting thicker tiles and narrow pieces of tile.

A simple carbide-tipped scoring tool is cheaper and will do the job as long as the tiles are not too thick, and not much cutting is involved.

Tile nippers, with tungsten-carbide jaws, are good for cutting small pieces of tile. They're easier to use on thick tiles than ordinary nippers.

A whetstone or file for smoothing edges of cut tiles.

Kitchen update
Tiles look luxurious and provide a durable surface that is easy to wipe clean. Here, bullnose trim tiles are used along kitchen countertop edges for a neat, professional finish.

CHECK YOUR NEEDS
- [ ] Tiles
- [ ] Trim tiles OR
      wood edging strip plus adhesive
      and finish nails
- [ ] Waterproof tile adhesive
- [ ] Notched adhesive spreader
- [ ] Tile spacers (for tiles without lugs)
- [ ] Tile cutter
- [ ] Tile nippers
- [ ] Whetstone or fine-toothed file
- [ ] Waterproof epoxy grout
- [ ] Flexible grout spreader or cloth
- [ ] Silicone sealant
- [ ] Furring strips or battens, about
      1 × 2in.
- [ ] Hammer
- [ ] Metal ruler
- [ ] Pencil and felt-tip pen
- [ ] Old cloths or sponge

1 *Plan the layout* ▽ ▷
Work out the best layout for tiling by loose-laying the whole surface and adjusting the tiles until they look right. If using square-edged tiles without lugs, fit tile spacers in between to allow for joints.

Keep cut tiles to the back of the countertop, and try to avoid narrow pieces of tile as they are difficult to cut.

The front edge How you finish the front edge of the countertop determines how you arrange the rest of the tiles.

If you're having a tiled edging (left), take into account the width of the trim tiles when laying out the whole tiles.

If you plan to have a wood edging (right), butt the whole tiles up to the front edge of the surface.

width

Tiling a rectangular shape Find and mark the center of the front edge of the countertop. Then match the center of a tile to this mark, and lay a row of loose tiles all along the front edge. If the countertop is open at both ends, adjust the tiles so that you have an equal border of cut tiles at each end. If it is open only at one end, place full tiles here and cut tiles along the walls.

Once the layout is fixed, mark the position of the center front row tile (*) as the starting point for tiling.

Tiling an L-shape For an L-shaped countertop, position a tile at the inside corner (*) and pencil around the edges to mark where tiling is going to start. As you cannot adjust the starting point, you may have to cut tiles to fit on exposed edges.

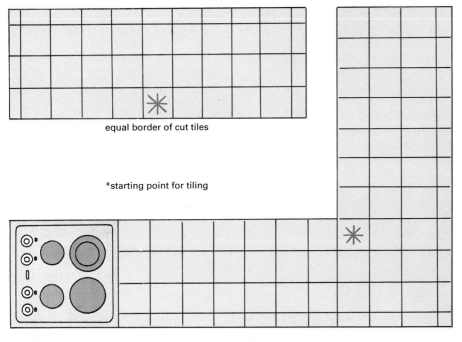

equal border of cut tiles

*starting point for tiling

2 *Prepare the base*
Wash down existing laminate or tiles, and rub over with sandpaper to provide a slightly rough surface for the new tile adhesive. Lift tiles that are loose or uneven and reset with new adhesive; fill any cracks and holes with all-purpose patching compound. Paint a new particle-board base with several coats of primer to seal it.

The front edge of the work surface should be the same depth as, or just less than, the depth of your chosen finish. If it's not, glue and screw a wood strip to the underside of the front edge, making sure that it doesn't obstruct any drawers or cupboard doors below.

3 *Begin with a straight edge* ▷
Use a wood strip along the front of the work surface as a guideline for positioning the first row of tiles in a straight line. Otherwise the layout is likely to end up askew.

If using a tiled edging (above right), mark a line along the front of the work surface to allow for the width of the trim tiles — these are laid last. Hold a straight piece of trim, short side vertical, against the edge of the work surface; make a series of pencil marks along the top edge of the tile and join them up with a straight line. Then loosely nail a wood strip up to the pencil line and use this as the edge for laying whole tiles.

With a wood edging (below right), tack the strip to the edge of the work surface so that it projects above the surface by the thickness of a tile.

4 *Start tiling ▷*
With your starting point in mind (see Step 1), apply enough adhesive with a notched spreader to lay four or five tiles along the front edge.

Lay the key tile (*) first, butting it against the furring strip, and press gently but firmly into place. Add the next tile alongside – butting edges together or fitting spacers if necessary – and continue along the row until you can't fit any more whole tiles. As you work, check that tiles are accurately aligned with each other; if the layout starts going askew and is not corrected, the error will get progressively worse.

5 *Add more tiles ◁*
Spread more adhesive and continue laying rows of full tiles, working back to the wall as far as you can go. Leave cut border tiles until last, but scrape off any adhesive in the area where they are going before it dries.

From time to time, press the tiles down with a furring strip as shown to make sure that the surface is level.

TILE SPACERS △
Substitute matchsticks for special tile spacers when laying square-edged tiles without lugs. Use two at each tile edge, and remove before grouting the joins.

6 *Mark border tiles*
Mark and cut border tiles individually to make sure that they fit the gaps between whole tiles and the wall, for example.

To mark a tile to fit, hold it glazed side down with one edge against the wall, and mark two points on the sides of the tile where the cutting line will be. Then turn the tile over and use a ruler and felt-tip pen to draw a line onto the glazed side.

7 *Cut border tiles*
Hold a metal ruler firmly against the cutting line and score along it deeply with a tile cutter.

Thick tiles, and very narrow pieces of tile, are best cut using a pair of tile snappers with angled jaws. Otherwise, put a matchstick under each end of the scored line and press firmly downwards on each side with your fingertips – if you feel resistance, score the line deeper and try again. If border

tiles are almost full-size, score a line in the usual way and nibble off the excess tile with nippers. Smooth rough edges with a whetstone or fine-toothed file.

Test each tile for fit, then spread adhesive onto the work surface and press the tile into place with the cut edge to the wall. If the space is narrow, it's often easier to apply adhesive to the back of the tile instead of the surface.

8 *Install the edging ▽*
Once the work surface has been completely tiled, remove the support and finish the edge with special trim tiles or with a length of wood molding.

A tiled edge Spread adhesive onto work surface and undersides of tiles, and position tiles so that joints align with those between whole tiles.

To lay the tiles, begin at an inside corner with the mitered tiles (below left). Then work out from the corner, laying the straight trim pieces (middle): if necessary, cut tiles to fit by scoring the surface deeply with a tile cutter and nibbling the waste away with nippers. At outside corners, use a special corner piece (right) – it may be necessary for you to cut a small piece

off the work surface to make the tile fit as neatly as possible.

A wood edge Cut molding to fit. Install with woodworker's glue and reinforce with finish nails, setting the heads and filling holes with wood putty. Follow Steps 9-11 next page, then seal wood with two or three coats of varnish or paint it to match the tiles.

9 Remove tile spacers
If you are using tile spacers (or matchsticks), leave the adhesive for an hour or two so that it sets firmly before prying them out carefully with a small screwdriver.

Rub off any adhesive on the tile surface with a damp cloth, taking care not to dislodge the tiles.

10 Apply the grout
Leave tiles for 24 hours before grouting. Using a flexible spreader or cloth, rub grout into the joints between tiles (except where horizontal tiles meet a sink or tiles on a wall).

Wipe off any splotches of grout on the tiles with a damp cloth before it dries, and run a small-diameter dowel along each joint to smooth the grout and leave the surface slightly concave. Leave grout to dry, then polish the tile surface with a soft dry cloth.

11 Use a sealant △
Use a flexible silicone sealant to seal the joint where tiles meet with a sink or basin, and to fill the gap between countertop and wall.

CUTTING AWKWARD SHAPES
Most cut tiles will have simple straight edges, but you may have to make a few odd-shape cuts to fit tiles around outside corners or around obstacles such as burner tops and sinks. Don't fit tiles too tightly around a burner top – allow a joint space as usual so that, as temperatures change, they can expand and contract without cracking.

Cutting a curve ▷
Make a tile-size template from cardboard or paper. Hold it in place against the curved object, and make a series of cuts in the edge with scissors or a sharp knife so that it can be folded to the shape of the curve.

Then cut the curved shape out of the cardboard, place the template on the tile and mark and score the outline. Score a grid of lines on the waste side of the line and nibble away small pieces with nippers until the line is reached. If necessary, smooth the cut edge with a whetstone or file.

Cutting L-shaped corner tiles △
Starting on one side of the corner, put the tile to be cut on top of the last whole tile laid before the wall. Then put another tile on top, but with its edge against the wall. Draw a cutting line across the middle tile, using the top one as a profile.

Slide the tiles around the corner and repeat on the other side of the angle. Join up the marked lines to form the L-shape and score them with a tile cutter. Then score a grid of lines over the waste area and nibble this away with nippers.

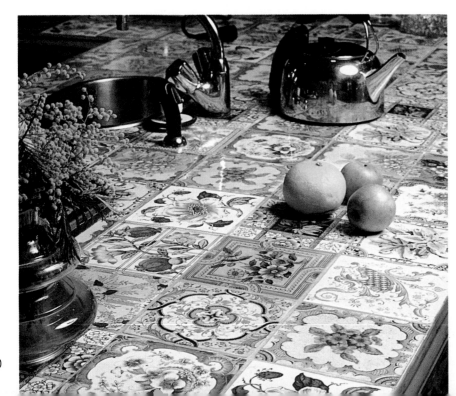

Patchwork picture ◁
An odd collection of tiles can be put together to great effect, as long as they're linked in some way – by color, pattern or style.

Here, a beautiful collection of antique tiles in warm, tawny colors makes a vivid patchwork of different floral designs on a kitchen countertop. Start collecting similar tiles by visiting tile shops, flea markets and antique dealers.

TILING A ROOM

Tiling large areas is no more difficult than small ones as long as you plan ahead carefully before you start.

The best way to practice your tiling skills if you've never tiled before is by covering just a small area such as a vanity backsplash or a countertop. See Basic Tiling Techniques and Tiling a Countertop, pages 83-90, for the basic techniques of planning out the area and installing, cutting and grouting tiles.

When you are tackling a larger area – a whole wall, or perhaps even a complete room – you use exactly the same techniques; the big difference is the sheer scale of the job, which makes the planning the most important part. The problem is that unless you have absolutely plain walls, there will be a number of obstacles to tile around. You have to decide how to get the best fit around them with the inflexible tile squares, without having to cut impossibly thin slivers to fill in all the gaps.

You may also want to tile awkward shapes such as the window recesses, or things like tub surrounds. Here, extra care is essential if you are to get professional-looking results.

Last, you may want to add decorative trims – wood, plastic or metal edgings, for example – to finish off your newly tiled areas. And then there's the problem of putting back the various wall-mounted fixtures that you had to take down to do the tiling in the first place.

TOOLS AND EQUIPMENT

You will need the same basic tools here as you did for tiling small areas – see Check Your Needs, page 92. In addition, for whole-wall tiling you will need some long straight wood battens to act as supports and guides, masonry nails plus a claw hammer to enable you to fit them temporarily to the walls, and a carpenter's level to ensure that the battens are fixed absolutely horizontal. You will also need a surprisingly large number of tiles for even quite a small wall. Measure accurately, counting all partial tiles as whole ones, and allowing 10% extra for mistakes. Also make sure that you have enough adhesive and grout to finish the job; nothing is more annoying than running out of adhesive with just a few tiles left to install. Always use waterproof adhesive and grout for moisture-prone wet areas such as kitchens and bathrooms.

Ceramic tiles have to be laid with joints between them to allow for expansion. Formerly this was achieved either by using tiles made with a small projection, or lug, on each side; or by inserting spacers while putting them up.

But many tiles nowadays are of the universal type, with no spacer lugs but beveled edges that serve the same purpose. They are glazed on two adjacent sides and so can be used at exposed edges or corners when necessary. The old-fashioned special tiles with one or two rounded and glazed edges (RE and REX tiles) are now seldom found.

Some less expensive tiles have edges that are erratically and poorly glazed, with just a few tiles in each box having two completely glazed edges. Keep this in mind if you need tiles with glazed edges of good quality for finishing off partially tiled walls and outside corners.

If you will have to drill holes in your new tiles to replace wall fixtures make sure you have sharp masonry drill bits, wall plugs and some masking tape to help you drill the holes accurately.

Strategic stripes
This well-planned tiling has striped tiles lining up with the sill line at the window and creating a baseboard effect at floor level. A wood trim in matching blue completes the picture.

PLANNING THE LAYOUT

If you're planning to tile or half-tile a complete wall or room, the most important thing to do is to plan precisely where the tiles will fall. You will need to look carefully at each wall and any features such as windows and doors to help you decide how to arrange the tiles.

A skilled tiler will use a batten marked out in tile widths to work this out, but for the beginner it's easier to use the actual tiles for a simple layout.

1 Planning a plain wall ▷
On a plain, uninterrupted wall this is quite straightforward. You start at the center bottom of the area to be tiled and work outwards and upwards from this point.

Measure across the wall and pencil on the center point. Center the first tile on this mark – either prop it against the wall or lay it on the floor. Lay out more tiles in each direction until you cannot get any more in. If the gaps left at each side are very small move the center mark to the left or right until they are at least one quarter of a tile wide. This is because narrow pieces not only look ugly but are very hard to cut. If your tiles are square-edged, insert slips of cardboard between them to represent the joint spacings.

2 Planning the vertical layout
Once you have established how the tiles are to run horizontally, check what's going to happen vertically. Hold a tile against one of the side walls at the baseboard or floor. Pencil tile widths up to the finishing point. If this results in an awkwardly narrow piece at the ceiling or the top row of half-tiling is not where you want it to be, use a cut tile at the bottom of the wall instead of a whole one.

3 Coping with a window ▷
If there is a window, center the tiles horizontally on it rather than the wall – some narrow pieces may be inevitable and are less conspicuous in corners. When planning the vertical layout, arrange the tiles so that whole tiles coincide with the sill level, but not if this means having very narrow cut pieces at the top. Repeat process on the other walls; take care to start from the same bottom line on each one.

PREPARING TO TILE

With large areas of tile, three things are vital. First, the walls must be sound and flat. Second, the tile rows must be precisely horizontal. If they're not, errors are compounded as you tile across the wall, throwing the verticals out of alignment with disastrous results. And if you're tiling completely around a room, inaccurate levels will mean that your rows won't match up at the starting and finishing points. Third, the tiles need some support while the adhesive sets. Without it the whole tiled area could slump down the wall.

1 Prepare the walls
To give a sound surface to tile over, strip off any wallcovering. Then fill any cracks and depressions with an all-purpose patching compound. Existing tiles can be tiled over provided that they are firmly stuck to the wall and the new joints come in different places.

2 Fix the battens ▷
To get the tiles horizontal, and to support them while the adhesive is drying, install a line of battens across the wall (or right around the room) just above baseboard or floor level, securing them with partly driven masonry nails so you can remove them later. The precise level will be dictated by your plan, but will usually be between half and three-quarters of a tile width above the baseboard or floor. Don't rely on these being level; they probably won't be. Draw the level in pencil first, using your carpenter's level, and then nail the battens up and check for level as you go.

3 Tiling over tiles
If you're tiling over existing tiles you will have to drill holes through them for the masonry nails that will hold the battens in place. Drill fine pilot holes in a batten, hold it up to the wall and drill through one batten hole into the tile. Nail this end in place, then swing the batten up, check it is horizontal with the carpenter's level and drill through its other end, ready for nailing.

TILING THE WALL

With all the battens in place you can start tiling.

1 *Find the starting point*
Refer to your pencil mark to see where your starting point is: the center of the wall, or some other point. Transfer the mark onto the batten. You can if you wish fit a vertical guide batten at one side, but it's not really necessary; a true horizontal base line will ensure that your verticals are true, too, so long as you place the tiles carefully.

2 *Apply the adhesive* ◁
Apply a band of adhesive to the wall and fit the first row of whole tiles, adding tile spacers at the top corners if necessary. Then continue up the wall, fitting whole tiles until you reach an obstacle such as a window opening. Continue tiling up the wall at each side of it, until you reach the top of half-tiling, or the last whole row of whole tiles beneath the ceiling. Remember to leave spaces for items such as soap dishes or for a mirror (see Bright Idea next page).

3 *Set in any trim*
If you're using a plastic or metal tile trim to finish off a half-tiled area, bed its rear flange in the adhesive before fitting the top row of tiles (see next page). Do not fit cut tiles at the side and top edges at this stage.

4 *Tile above openings* ▷
Where tiles are to be fixed over a recessed window opening, you will need another support batten. Attach it to the wall over the opening with its top edge in line with the top edge of the whole tiles you placed earlier at each side of the opening. Then continue tiling as before, placing whole tiles up to ceiling level. Leave all the battens in place for at least 24 hours to allow the adhesive to set hard.

5 *Fit the cut tiles* ◁
Next day, carefully pry out the masonry nails holding the battens in place, using a claw hammer, and remove the battens. Pry out any tile spacers at this stage too. Mark and cut tiles to fit the space between the baseboard or floor and fix them in position. It's easier to spread adhesive on the back of each cut piece with the notched spreader than to try to apply it to the narrow section of exposed wall.

Then fit cut tiles at each side of the wall, and between the last row of whole tiles and the ceiling if the tiling is full height, positioning the cut edge of each tile against the ceiling.

If you have tiled more than one wall, fill in the cut pieces on each wall. Make sure that there is a slight gap between adjacent cut corner pieces to allow for any slight movement in the house structure. If the pieces are a tight fit this could crack them.

6 *Tile window recesses* ◁
The next step is to tile any window recesses, shelves or boxes concealing pipework. Start by cutting tiles to fit the gap left on the face of the wall between the last row of whole tiles and the edges of the recess. Then fix whole tiles to the sill, sides and top of the opening so their glazed edges neatly overlap the cut edges of the tiles you just placed. If the recess is shallow,

cut the tiles at the back edges to fit. If you are tiling the 'ceiling' or top of the window recess, you may need to rig up a temporary support – a batten and props wedged between top and sill – to support the tiles. Finally, on a deep recess, fit cut pieces between the whole tiles and the window frame to complete the recess.

7 *Tiling outside corners* ◁
A similar overlap to the one around a window recess is formed at outside corners. The rule here is to have the tile with the exposed, glazed edge on the more prominent wall.

If you are tiling three adjacent surfaces – on a fully tiled, boxed-in tub surround, for example – the overlap at the outside corner cannot be accommodated without a gap equal to the thickness of a tile being left on

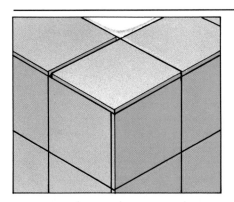

the top. This will not be noticeable when filled with grout. Position the tiles as shown in the diagram, so that the horizontal corner tile covers the edges of the top two vertical tiles laid below it.

FINISHING THE JOB

After all the tiling has been completed, the trim, grout and accessories have to be added to give the finishing touches to the job.

1 Add the trim

As mentioned earlier, you can finish off tiled areas and outside corners neatly with special plastic or metal tile trims that give a neat, rounded edge. Cut them to length with a fine-toothed hacksaw, mitering the corners in a miter box if framing a window casing or similar opening. Bed the trim in the tile adhesive before placing the final row of tiles over the trim's back flange and carefully tap the trim in place so it sits flush with the tile edges.

2 Add accessories ▷

If you are adding matching ceramic accessories such as soap dishes and toilet roll holders, leave spaces in the field tiles and wipe away the adhesive. Next day, when fitting the cut tiles, spread some adhesive onto the back of the accessory and set it in place. Use masking tape to support it while the adhesive 'grabs'.

3 Grout the tiles

Allow the adhesive to set overnight. Then grout all the gaps using a flexible plastic spreader. Wipe off excess grout with a damp cloth as you work, and round off the grout lines with a piece of narrow dowel. When the grout is dry, polish the tile

surfaces with a clean dry cloth to remove smears.

It's best not to grout inside corners since movement in the house structure could cause cracking. Use silicone sealant instead, which remains flexible.

4 Replace fixtures

If you have screw-mounted wall fixtures such as mirrors and shelves to replace once tiling is complete, stick masking tape to the tile surface and mark the fixture positions on it. The tape prevents the drill bit from skating away from the mark. Use a sharp masonry drill bit and a slow speed

setting on the drill, pressing lightly until the bit bites through the tile glaze. Then drill the hole to the required depth. Remove the tape, insert the wall plug and attach the fixture. In a really wet area such as a shower cubicle put a bead of silicone sealant around the screw shank as you drive it in to stop water from seeping behind the tiles.

BRIGHT IDEA

Hanging a mirror If you want to have mirrors in the bathroom you can simply screw them to the tiled wall with mirror screws. The only drawback is that steam can affect the silvering if it reaches the back of the mirror. To get around this, fit the mirror flush with the tiles. To assure a perfect fit (and save the tiles) leave a space for the mirror when laying the tiles, then measure the area and order a mirror of that size from a glass dealer. Stick it to the wall with adhesive pads or blobs of epoxy adhesive. Seal the joint between mirror and tiles with silicone sealant. Stick masking tape to the edges of the mirror while applying the sealant to it so that you don't smear the surface.

◁ *Decorative backsplash*
A tiled backsplash can add a colorful personal touch to any kitchen. Not only is it practical, it becomes the focal point of the cooking area. Painted tiles must be carefully set so that the end result is neat and properly aligned.

INDEX

PHOTOGRAPHIC CREDITS

Aristocast, 68
Jean-Paul Bonhommet, 60
Simon Butcher/Eaglemoss, 32, 40
Cover Plus from Woolworths, 56
Cristal Tiles, 87, 91
Crown Paints, 24 (inset), 48, 53, 69, 72
Dorma, 21, 23
Dulux, 2-3, 6, 7, 13, 17, 36, 41, 45, 75
Phillip H. Ennis Photography, 2-3
EWA/A von Einsiedel, 25
EWA/Jerry Tubby, 90
EWA/Michael Dunne, 57, 66
EWA/Spike Powell, 51
EWA/Tom Leighton, 33
La Maison de Marie Claire/Eriaud/Comte, 29

Barbara Ostrom Associates, front cover interior designer
Freda Parker/Eaglemoss, 37
Parsekian/Gensheimer, front cover photograph
PWA International, 16, 61, 78
Slatkin & Company, interior designer, 2-3
Stencil Ease at Carolyn Warrender, 49
Stencil-itis, 1
Chris Stephens/Eaglemoss, 23, 24
Summitville Tiles Studio, 94
Steve Tanner/Eaglemoss, 4-5
Sara Taylor/Eaglemoss, 83
Textra, 79, 82
Mr. Tomkinson, 42
Winchmore Ltd., 86
Shona Wood/Eaglemoss, 28